AS YOU STEP INTO TEACHING

9 Perspectives for a Purpose-Driven Teaching

Joenel Dicen Coros

ISBN 979-8-89485-222-5 (Paperback)
ISBN 979-8-89485-223-2 (Digital)

Covenant Books
11661 Hwy 707
Murrells Inlet, SC 29576
www.covenantbooks.com

CONTENTS

PREFACE

After eleven years of teaching, I found a tool that could help teachers, especially the starting ones, that could guide them in their practice. It dawned on me when I started to teach in the "land of the free and home of the brave" ('cause, you know, I'm "free" and "brave"). First year—I was very excited to bring everything I know to the school and to my classroom, but when I took over, all of it seemed to be just phantasms. To teach in this land for a "first year" is not that easy. There is one thing I was certain though: My students were acting according to their age and nature, and *I do not know* how to handle them! Then questions like

- "Do all first-year teachers have this experience?"
- "Is this experience the same for all teachers?" and
- "Is this just happening to me?"

The questions kept hanging on my head, urging me to find solutions.

Many times, I tried to step back in the classroom and observe my students. I also observed them with other teachers and school staff—how they interact inside and outside of other classrooms. I have seen how they would comply with assignments when there are rewards. I have seen how they respond with corrections. I have seen how they could be playful and not when with their peers. My observations simply confirm to me that *they are just kids doing things as kids*. (But why do I find it hard to handle them?)

The urge to find solutions even got stronger in me when a colleague of mine asked himself, "Do I really know how to teach? What is wrong with what I am doing? I am already doing all the best I can." It struck me. I can feel him, for at one point, I asked myself the same questions (and who knows how much more are asking the same questions). I was very fortunate, however, for I have an amazing school principal, school administrators, coach, teaching team, content partner, and colleagues who were constantly there to support me. My year was filled with so much learning.

Throughout the year, I studied materials, played with strategies, observed other teachers, tried approaches, reflected on my practices and experiences, and considered all factors that play around my students. My rationale was simple: "If I could figure things out, then I could better teach my students" (and perhaps share it to others in the future, especially those who will step into the teaching world for the first time in this land). As the months went through, I have seen changes in the general behavior of my students in the classroom—from chaos to calm, from off-task to on-task, and from disengagement to engagement. I won't deny that there remained daily challenges, but I have felt the "difference." Most importantly, I have found a very useful tool that every teacher, especially the starting ones, could hold on to to feel the significant changes in their classroom: *perspective*—our way of looking at and understanding things.

When we look at things at different angles, heights, and characters, our place in the vast dynamic ecology of education and the answer to why we do what we do every day gets unraveled. Seeing the perspectives, I believe that teachers can better their practice, subconsciously working on what they aspire for each of their students—the *love for learning*.

To Teach Is to Serve

Teachers came to serve, not to be served.

Literally, Teachers Are Servants

If you can't be a servant, you can't be a teacher. This is the reason why some people are not attracted to the teaching profession and why some of the younger generations don't aspire to be teachers. To be a servant means to choose to belong to the "lowest social class" and be a "jack of all trades." [i,ii] This has been true in history up to this day.

To be a servant, to belong to the lowest social class, requires free will. Servants are "hired individuals."[iii] This is what makes them different from a slave. This means that they may choose to leave the job when they don't find it rewarding anymore. The people who can't be a servant, especially if he has huge dreams for himself, for his family, and for all the people around him, know that a "teaching job" may not probably be the good route to achieve it. One example of this is when I asked my students.

"What was your dream when you were younger?" I asked.

"Uhmmm…when I was younger, I wanted to be a teacher," she responded.

"Wanted…what do you mean by that?"

She replied, "I changed my mind. I learned that teachers don't get paid much. I want to be an architect instead."

(Sad but true.)

I asked a similar question to another student.

"Given the chance, would you ever want to become a teacher?"

My student responded, "No…teachers don't get paid much, and their job is hard."

(Truly)

There are many other instances where I learned from my students and from all other people around me that they find teaching a low-esteemed profession. There is nothing wrong with what they see, and I have no objection to what they are saying. After all, that is true. It is true that teachers are perceived to belong to the lowest social class. It is true that teachers don't get paid well. It is true that teachers have a hard job.

How about those who, for some reason, fell into the teaching profession out of their free will? This is the answer: "If they can't be a servant, they can't be a teacher." This is the same with those who cannot sustain the challenges of teaching. It's just a matter of time—they will eventually choose to leave. Servants are not slaves; they have free will.

The Good Servant

What is a good servant?

Let us answer this question with the help of the parable of Two Sons.

> There was a man who had two sons. He went to the first and said, "Son, go and work today in the vineyard." "I will not," he answered, but later he changed his mind and went. Then the father went to the other son and said the same thing. He answered, "I will, sir," but he did not go.[iv]

I've been a teacher for more than a decade now, and I am certain that good teachers are like the first son. They might say "I will not," but their actions will prove otherwise. Their obedience is through their actions.

But what draws the line between the good servant and that which is not? Respect.

This reminds me of the words of John Maxwell—that there are two acid tests to determine if someone has respect for a leader: First, "the response of people when you ask for commitment." Second, "the response of people when a leader asks them to change."[v] The first son changed his mind and went, for he has respect to his father. The second son just affirmed, but there was really no intention to do what the father asked in the first place.

A good servant is a respectful servant.

The Heart of a Good Servant

A good servant is a respectful servant. His respect can be seen through his actions—how he follows through with what his higher authority would ask of him. If respect is a demonstration of the servant's heart, what then is in the heart of a servant?

Humility

Respect is a demonstration of humility. Humility is the capability of one person to swallow his pride after thoughtful consideration, as shown in the parable:

> "I will not," he answered, but later he changed his mind and went.

Without this quality, the first son could not have gone to do what his father asked of him. To have humility takes a lot of character, for it requires a person to have a down-to-earth view about the situations. This view can be attributed to three things about a person: *security, experience, and competence.*

1. *Security.* People with humility are secure people. They are not afraid of what other people will say about their actions. They deeply understand that in everything they do, people will always have something to say; and so, they are not swayed. They just do what they believe is right. I have seen this demonstrated during my first year.

   It was the rainy season during my actual first year of teaching. My classroom was different from the conventional ones because I had with me three other teachers teaching other different subjects. This is because our students were learning various subjects and on different pages at the same time. Simply, they are learning the subjects "at their own pace."

As usual, we were doing our jobs—going here and there, answering students' academic questions, and supporting the students with what they need. Then at one point, dripping water appeared from the ceiling of the classroom which, perhaps, was because there was so much more stored up in the ceiling that we didn't know. It later busted and flooded the room. It was a mess.

I was surprised when suddenly the one who responded was in formal attire, holding a bucket and a mop, and he mopped the floors. It was our boss—the highest official in our school. Seeing him taking care of that mess in the classroom, all of us helped by getting rags, putting it on the floors, and even squeezing the water it collects into the bucket. I will never forget that. Instead of calling for one of his workers to clean it up, as he was the boss after all, he had put his hands first.

2. *Experience.* Humility usually comes from hard experiences. People with humility deeply understand, for they know too well how it feels to be at the bottom of life, of a situation. They can relate, for usually they have been there. Hence, once they see anyone in a really hard situation, they can see themselves in that person. They acknowledge as well that they can do no more than support that person in as much as they can, for they understand the value of experience. There is no way to become a better person, a person of broader view and deeper wisdom, but through it.

I have seen this demonstrated by my instructional coach during my eleventh year in teaching. I was teaching seventh-grade science, so I have faucets and sinks around my classroom. There was one instance where one student sneaked to turn on the faucet, which resulted in flooding a section of the room. At that same time, my coach came in, and what he did was simply turned off the faucet, get a mop and paper towels, and clean it up. I was shocked, then I apologized for not seeing it earlier, but I was responded with "No, you're fine." If my coach was someone who never had that experience, he might not be able to relate, and perhaps how the situation would turn out might be different. I don't know.

3. *Competence.* People with humility are usually the most competent people. They are competent, yet they seem not to know it. I believe that this is because they know that what they know remains too little before the vastness of the knowledge that the world offers. They are humbled each time they learn. They are consistently in a quest to learn new things, making them knowledgeable in many aspects, making them skillful, making them competent in their field. However, the more they learn, the more they realize that they know so little. The more they learn, the more they are humbled. Throughout history to the present time, you will find this true. The most competent people are the humblest people.

Integrity

Integrity was demonstrated by the first son in the parable. Though the son said he didn't want to work as his father told him, he later changed his mind and went. He chose to do what he was told. He chose to do what was right even when his father did not convince him any further. Described by a coach Elizabeth Perry,

> A person with integrity behaves ethically, and does the right thing, even behind closed doors.[vi]

A teacher with the heart of a servant will always do what is right, for he considers what is good for the many.

They don't work to impress. Whether they will be recognized or not, they don't mind. They deeply understand that their goal is to contribute to the achievement of the greater good—the good that will work on the students, the community, the school, the district, the state, and the educational system. They work with the end in the mind that their role is vital to the fulfillment of the greater good.

Stewardship

Teachers with the heart of a servant know their place in the educational system. They deeply understand the vitality of their role in that system, and so they do their part, at their best. They understand that they are the caretakers of everything that's in their classroom for the generations of students and teachers who will come after them. They understand that their students will come and go, and so while they are in their room, they will do their best to protect them from any harm and take care of them. They acknowledge the fact that when the time comes that their role is over in the classroom, another teacher will take over their room and continue the things they have once been doing.

The Greatest Demonstration

There is no other greater demonstration I know of about having a heart of a servant than this:

> He got up from the meal, took off his outer clothing, and wrapped a towel around his waist. After that, he poured water into a basin and began to wash his disciples' feet, drying them with the towel that was wrapped around him… When he had finished washing their feet, he put on his clothes and returned to his place.[vii]

There is no demonstration greater than this. It was like my boss—putting aside his position to grab a mop and clean up flooded floor, serving us and my students. It was like my coach—putting aside his title and experience, cleaning up the flooded floor caused by a sneaky student, and addressing the behavior in a calm manner. I have seen these many times from all others—a principal picking up trash, a supervisor bringing the supplies for her teachers, a group of teachers preparing a stage decoration, lifting chairs, and cleaning up the venue for a program prepared for the parents, students, and other stakeholders, and so on. Hence, whatever degree we may attain, how many years of teaching experience we may have, we should ground ourselves on the demonstration of the greatest teacher of all.

Teachers came to serve, not to be served.

PERSPECTIVE 2

Strive to Grow

*What your students can know and do is influenced
by what you know and can do.*

We Are Gifted to Learn

The ability to grow in learning is deeply knitted in mankind's DNA since the beginning of time. We naturally learned to crawl, to stand, to walk, to run, to speak, etc. We were gifted with the ability to learn and pursue our interests—should we desire to. Even when we look back to primitive times, we learned to read the weather, learned the patterns of behavior of animals, learned to use fire for so many applications, discovered medicinal plants on their own, learned the strength of being together, and so on. It rolled on and on that in the passing of time, all the learnings we had led to mankind's progress and development.

We are the only creatures gifted with the ability to achieve unimaginable possibilities should we take courage to initiate and pursue it—the only creature capable of discovering, inventing, and creating, the only creature gifted with the capability to change his fate should he desire to anytime he wants, the only creatures gifted with the power to influence all other creations should we choose to break through the self-imposed barriers toward personal development and choose to get better day by day into becoming and joining the leaders of the pack. We are very special to be the only creatures gifted with the ability to learn remarkable things—anything that we want to—for life.

Mindset Makes the Difference

In my early years in the profession, I used to criticize the system for not giving the teachers sufficient opportunities to attend seminars, get trained, and learn more. For if they can learn more, they can be more. Curriculums are changing, the behavior of students is changing, the level of support of parents is changing, everything in the educational system is changing but the teacher's knowledge and skills seem to remain the same. What we know from college graduation seems to be the same after having served the system for ten, twenty, thirty years! If there is any addition to it, it's so little compared to the magnitude of learnings that we had in our student life.

Then you would hear frustrations about all this stuff—curriculum, students, parents, administrative support, and so on.

Why is that?

Perhaps because we need to meet our dreams and aspirations that can be granted to us by working day in and day out by our employer? Or maybe because after graduation, we felt compelled to assume commitments and responsibilities in the family that were not initially upon our shoulders? Or probably there are personal matters that happened to us after graduation that we must direct and devote our time to it?

This I tell you: "They are not."

We have conditioned ourselves. We have conditioned ourselves that to be a student ends when we have earned our diploma—undergraduate, master's, doctorate, whichever level we have achieved at most. We conditioned ourselves to think that we were only students on the four walls of the classroom. We have conditioned ourselves that we are only a student when we have that enrollment form in a school or a university. After all, we have been doing that year after year during our student life. Because of that self-conditioning, we forgot our nature—that we are gifted with the ability to learn "anything" if we desire to. We have conditioned ourselves to forget our very nature—that we can learn even if there is no training or seminar initiated by the district or division, that we can be a student of the profession we chose, that we are capable of achieving remarkable things.

We have conditioned ourselves to impose limits on our minds. We have conditioned ourselves to have that mindset. All these things are the opposite of our very nature. Consider these three cardinal rules of a "growth mindset" *(the nature of our mindset that we forgot)* offered to us by Stanford psychology professor Carol Dweck:

1. Learn, learn, learn!
2. Work with passion and dedication—effort is the key.
3. Embrace your mistakes and confront your deficiencies.[viii]

First, we have conditioned ourselves that we are only a student upon enrollment and when we are associated to a school or a university. Second, the world is so huge that our efforts do not have the power to influence its dynamics, and so why bother to exert? Third, we have conditioned ourselves not to take risks, stay in our comfort zone, complain and criticize about the things that are not within our influence. We conditioned ourselves to become the exact opposite of our nature. Therefore, it is our mindset that makes the difference; hence, it is also our mindset that can make the difference.

Why Should We Strive to Grow?

A teacher influences the learning capacity and capability of his students. This is not an opinion but an empirical truth that may be confirmed in the literature.[ix] If a teacher has a mindset that settles to stunt and comfort, so his students can be. If a teacher has the perspective of endless possibilities, so his students can be. If a teacher puts value on growth, diligence, and persistence, so his students can be. If a teacher possesses a strong character, so his students can be. In other words, every capability of the students—or his inability—can be influenced by the teachers he has had.

So be the reason why your students have the skills to learn anything they want that they may be anyone they want and that they may be able to reach their stars and the desires of their heart. Be the reason why they have the courage to go out of their comfort zone and explore the unfamiliar forest of uncertainties toward their personal development and fulfillment. Be the reason that they can stretch beyond their self-imposed limits.

The Four Kinds of Teachers

There are four kinds of teachers, who can be characterized when they are offered with new knowledge or faced with a new challenge. They are as follows:

1. *Prideful Teacher.* He knows everything about teaching. His cup is full.

2. *Pessimistic Teacher.* He entertains the knowledge shared to him about teaching but is in doubt about it. He might try to bring that knowledge to practical use but when met with some setbacks, he easily gives it up. He has inadequate patience and persistence.

3. *Undisciplined Teacher.* He believes in the knowledge shared to him about teaching, and he puts it into practical use, but he is not growing at best. There are inner issues that he needs to resolve and environmental factors that hampers his growth. He lacks self-discipline, confidence, and support.

4. *Growing Teacher.* He is the one who believes the knowledge about teaching, who brings it to practical use, and who is growing at best. This kind of teacher is constantly learning and practicing. He has a growth mindset, is adequately supported, and delivers impact to everyone around them.

The Growing Teacher

The growing teachers are the fourth kind of teacher—they are equipped with the knowledge and wisdoms of teaching, they bring it to practical use, and they are constantly growing at best. More than the mindset they have, they deliver impact to those around them. Their mindset is operated by Carol Dweck's cardinal rules for a growth mindset:

Learn! Learn! Learn!
Work with passion and dedication—effort is the
 key, and
Embrace your mistakes and confront your
 deficiencies.

What do the rules mean?
The first rule implies *continuity.* The perspective is that learning is like a line that goes to infinity, not a segment that has a stopping point. The rule defies age, ability, and even intelligence—in

other words, not because you have reached a certain age, not because you don't have the ability or little ability, and not because your intelligence falls on a particular spectrum; that's the limit of what you can know and do.

The second rule emphasizes the importance of *practice*. The perspective is that you cannot sharpen what you do not sharpen. The rule suggests that knowing is different from doing. Knowing is important for it is foundational, but doing it is even more important for you are able to use what you know to practical use. The rule encourages anyone to put themselves into a regimen of "doing" to get better on what they do.

The third rule teaches us *conquering*. The perspective is that trying to grow in learning is like being in a war. It is a long-term fight. There are battles where you will win, and there are battles where you will lose. The rule tells us that to conquer, you must get up each time you lose. Identify your weaknesses, and work on it. Accept losses, but don't let those losses stop you from winning the war. This means that you have a clear recognition that the way to figure out things is to keep finding ways to figure out no matter how many times you might have felt defeated.

The Barriers of Growth

If we want to grow, we should recognize what may hinder us from doing so. Looking back to the four kinds of teachers, we can find the issues that we need to resolve for each of them. For the first one, it is pride. For the second, it is inadequate patience, hence, persistence. For the third, it is the lack of self-discipline and confidence in himself. Let us talk about them one by one.

Pride

Pride is the greatest enemy of growth. Humility is its best friend. If we want to be a teacher who is growing, constantly thirsty and hungry for learning, we should not put our position, degree, and experience in our head. By acknowledging that what we know is just a drop in the vast ocean of knowledge before us, we could get tied to the truth that we have nothing to boast. Then the inner drive to know more kicks in, unconsciously becoming more. "Learn, learn, learn!"—one of the cardinal rules for growth mindset to operate. Put your pride in the corner of the room, for as the saying goes:

> Empty your cup so that it may be filled;
> become devoid to gain totality.[x]

Inadequate Patience, Hence, Persistence

A teacher with inadequate patience easily gives up trying—for himself and for his students. He fails to recognize that growth takes time, that a seed you planted today does not become a tree by tomorrow. Patience is the core of persistence. To persist means to keep going—and going and going—until you penetrate a seemingly adamant barrier. In the words of Roman poet Ovid,

> Dripping water hollows out stone, not
> through force, but persistence.[xi]

Patient teachers maintain that positive attitude while waiting for the bulb up his student's head to finally light up. A patient teacher understands that overcoming takes time, that learning takes time. Put the other way around, how far a teacher can persist is an indicator of the depth of his patience.

Lack of Self-Discipline

Self-discipline is the core of growth. Self-discipline is not just about sticking to a routine of exercise to maintain your health or to achieve a body shape you aspire. More than that, it is about training the mind and the body to do what is right over what is convenient—all the time. As described by Jim Rohn, "Discipline means doing what needs to be done even when you feel like not doing it."[xii] Teachers who lack self-discipline are the third kind of teachers. They know a lot about teaching. They put what they know to practical use for the most part. However, they sometimes deliberately allow what is convenient to triumph over what is right—"deliberate" in the sense that they failed to discipline the "self" in doing what is right. They allowed what is convenient to triumph over what is right.

Weak Self-Confidence

The fourth barrier of growth is weak self-confidence. If you worry about other people's opinion of you, you will be a teacher who is constantly in doubt of your ideas. While we must acknowledge feedback and criticisms as wonderful piece of information and insights, they should not be the benchmark on what we should accept to be good—for our practice, for our classroom, for our students, for our community.

For as long as you know that what you're doing is right, well-intentioned, beneficial, geared toward excellence, does not go against school and district policies, does not go against the laws of the land and divine laws—however you may call it, just do it. Just do it. Don't fear what your leader or administrators will think of you. This is what I know about them: "Once they see you trying, they will support you all the way!" So keep trying. If you fail, learn from it. If you succeed, celebrate. As an adage had said,

> It's better to regret trying and failing than
> to regret not trying at all.[xiii]

Let no one's opinion stop you from showing your true self as a teacher. Do not be a kind of teacher who is imprisoned by other people's opinion.

Your Thoughts Measure Your Growth

There is no limit to how much you can learn unless you conceive it. When you begin to believe that a "limit exists," your mind will eventually believe it. You will come up to all the "reasons" and "excuses" why you may not be able to go beyond to what more you can do when you reach the wall of your understanding and capabilities. If you believe the other way around, that limits are nonexistent, that there is a way to get through every wall, you will gain the perspective of "endless possibilities" for any situation or circumstance. "Thoughts are things," as Napoleon Hill said[xiv]—if you believe it, then it's true—second to this the words of Henry Ford that goes "Whether you think you can or think you can't, you're right."[xv] Hence, your thoughts measure your growth.

Think about the figures in every field—sports, entertainment, professions, or perhaps the people closest to us that we consider "topnotch," "great," or "champion." They were able to surpass talents, abilities, and capabilities that the average failed to achieve, for they recognize this truth. The limits of what they can know and do depends on them, and so they fight all the reasons and excuses that hinders them to get through their wall of understanding and capabilities. They find ways. They step forward. They explore the uncharted course. They go miles beyond what others may not reach. While others stopped, they persisted. This is what sets them apart from the average. They know that their growth will only stop when they choose to.

This truth applies to you as a teacher. There is no limit to what you can understand and be capable of unless you conceive it. Your thoughts can measure your growth. You can grow as much as you want in the profession. You can learn as much as you want about anything that you choose to be better—classroom management, teaching strategies, curriculum, assessment, technologies, partnership with the parents, working with the community, and all others. It is just a matter of how far you want to know, do, and go. For as long as you have the wonderings and you have that burning desire to get though them, you could always do so. You are always capable of understanding and learning new things.

You can always choose to grow.

PERSPECTIVE 3

Aspire for "Flow"

Setting the flow conditions is the key to engagement.

Why Aspire for "Flow"?

First, let's talk about "engagement." According to Phillip Schlechty, a student's engagement may be characterized with their "attention" and "commitment" then categorized into five levels: "rebellion," "retreatism," "ritual compliance," "strategic compliance," and "engagement."[xvi] A student that is "engaged" has "high attention" and "high commitment." When engaged,

> Students associates the task with a result or a product that has meaning or value for them. They will persist in the face of difficulty and drive their own learning.[xvii]

Hence,

> Students who are engaged: learn at high levels and have a profound grasp of what they learn; retain what they learn; and can transfer what they learn to new contexts.[xviii]

"Flow," in Mihaly Csikszentmihalyi's words, is

> The state in which people are so involved in an activity that nothing else seems to matter; the experience itself is so enjoyable that people will do it even at greater cost, for the sheer sake of doing.[xix]

This means that when someone is in a state of flow, he is engaged "totally." "Flow is the peak experience of engagement."[xx] This is also described as being "in the zone."[xxi] In this state, "creativity is shown to increase 500 to 700 percent," enabling us to "take in more information faster," "link together ideas more readily," and "connect more ideas readily."[xxii] Hence, if we are to aim for student engagement, we must understand the conditions for flow. As stated by Carol Whitson and Jodi Consoli,

> Attaining flow, or coming near to attaining flow, may increase positive learning outcomes associated with increased student engagement.[xxiii]

But what are the conditions for flow that gives way to student engagement?

Three Conditions for Flow

In the study of David Shernoff and others, they have found three conditions, innumerably: "instructions should be relevant," "learning environment is under control," and "challenge and skills are in balance."[xxiv] In the succeeding sections, they are correspondingly explained as "Clarity of Goals," "Clarity of Behavior Expectations," and "Balance of Challenge and Skills."

Clarity of Goals

Why are we doing what we are doing? That's the question being answered by the goal. It can be the daily goal, weekly, unit, or end-of-the-year goal. This reminds me of an experience I had. In our school district, we are given an opportunity to go to other school and observe classes. After observing four classes, I have found similar practices among the teachers that I find contributory to student engagement. Let me share to you the reflection I wrote in that observation:

> The use of planners, the use of timers in each segment of the lesson, the employment of note-taking strategies—these made an impression on me during observations that the students have a sense of what has been and where they are going. In a phrase, they have a "Sense of Self-

Direction." I believe that this sense of self-direction leads to improved student engagement.

The teachers employed strategies to help students achieve the goal, and the students developed the skill of goal setting. The students know why they do what they do—from the day before to the present day to the next day—all because there was clarity of goals.

Clarity of Behavior Expectations

Setting clear expectations is vital for flow, for it seeks to eliminate distractions, giving way to optimal learning environment, subsequently to a heightened experience of engagement.

As a teacher, we sometimes fall on the guilt trap not to enforce negative consequences especially to our challenging students. Let us not. This reminds me of a time I saw a mother disciplining her kid. Her husband was there, watching, then later told her that her words are already hurtful to their son. Then she replied, "Do you think I don't have a heart? Do you think that I don't get hurt whenever I need to correct our son?" It silenced her husband. Indeed, love corrects. It might hurt you as a teacher, but there are times when you just need to really enforce the negative consequences when your expectations are challenged by your students. A challenge in your expectation is a challenge in your authority in the classroom. If you fail to address it, your authority will corrode.

Balance of Challenge and Skills

Simply explained, the challenge level should match one's skill level to be in the flow state. If the challenge and the skill don't match, it may result to anxiety or boredom. Illustrated below is how state of flow may be experienced according to Mihaly Csikszentmihalyi:[xxv]

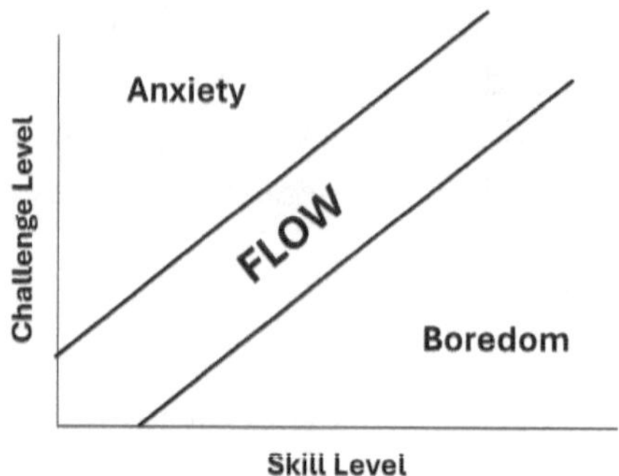

During class, you can easily determine where your students are in terms of flow or not. If the challenge is too high and the skill level is too low, they show anxiety, frustration, and an attitude of giving up. Here you might hear a complaining and whining phrase from your students like "This is too hard!"

"I can't do this!"

"This is too much!"

On the other hand, if the challenge is too low and the skill is too high, it may result to individual's boredom. The individual may find it too easy and may even find it meaningless to work on. Here you might see students getting off-task or doing something else. When asked, you may get a low energy response of "I'm bored."

"I know this already."

"I already learned this when I was..."

These situations are an everyday reality and a challenge to every teacher since the classroom is filled with students whose need for the challenge falls in various sections of the academic spectrum. This is where differentiation, student-choice on assignment, and isolated support would emerge as potential solutions. Nevertheless, understanding the balance of challenge and skills as one necessary condition for flow informs the teacher of potential reasons when he finds some of his students getting frustrated or bored. It will make the teacher think of ways to adjust his lessons so that he may drag or push his students to a state of flow.

To sum it up, there are three flow conditions that teachers must consider in the design of his instructions: "Clarity of Goals," "Clarity of Behavior Expectations," and "Balance of Challenge and Skills." The purpose of clarity of goals is to direct students' effort into the reason, the "why" of their efforts. Clarity of expectations addresses classroom distractions by making the teacher and students have a common language and understanding of what is allowed and not in the classroom. Balance of challenge and skills addresses the "appropriateness" of challenge level in relation to the student's skill level.

Three Keys for Engagement

The three conditions for flow will help us set our students up for engagement. Those conditions were set to allow optimal learning environment to happen, but when they are already in place, what's next? How can we make engagement happen? Or maybe the better question is what are the keys to unlock student engagement?

Let us answer this question with the help of its definition. In engagement,

> Students associates the task with a result or
> a product that has meaning or value for them.
> They will persist in the face of difficulty and
> drive their own learning.[xxvi]

To emphasize, "if the task leads to a result or product that has a meaning or value to them," they will "drive their own learning," and they will "persist in the face of difficulty." It looks like this:

Intrinsic Value of Task → Inner Drive to
Accomplish + Persistence in Difficulty

Now, what is that which has an "intrinsic value" to a student?

Consider the four situations I have found out of the context:

1. *The Dentist.* It was Saturday morning when I had an appointment with my dentist. We had a good conversation about how I ended up in teaching and how am I doing with my job. At one point, he shared that he tried to teach in a medical school, but he seemed to not love what he was doing. Not happy with the job, he tried to enroll in dentistry where he felt the enjoyment of being on it, and so he pursued. It struck me when he said, "You know, it's easier to learn when it's fun." Those words stuck in my head: "It's easier to learn when it's fun."

2. *Kids at Play.* One Saturday, I was sitting on a chair, watching my two kids as they play who is the dentist, then one would volunteer who will be the patient. There are findings of "Oh, your tooth got broken because you are eating so much candy," so here we go with procedures, prescriptions, and the doctor will eventually say, "You'll be fine." After that, they will switch roles and just do it all over again. Nobody told them to do that, but they had "fun" doing that play of switching with the dentist-patient role.

3. *Research Presentations.* Back in the Philippines, I handle a subject, "practical research," where its culminating activity is for students to bring their manuscript and products and present it before a panel of evaluators. In its conception stage, they are to find a problem in the community that they need to solve and conduct a review of literature about it toward finding the solution. They set their goal, make plans, find people who could help them, find the materials they need on their own, send letters and ask permission from some agencies, and so on. During the presentation, there are instances where they would share stories on the difficulties they encountered, would laugh at some experiences but, most importantly, how they succeeded with solving the problems they initially identified evidenced by their completed manuscript and product.

Obviously, the drive to learn, play, and create a product came from the inner self. In other words, they were *not forced* to do the things and the doing of things *do not feel punitive* but *enjoying*, for it seems like they are just *playing*.

In the same light, not all students have the same inclination. Howard Gardner reminds us of this, the multiple intelligences.[xxvii] Usually, though, we are tempted to ask our students of a one-size-fits-all output. A story worth mentioning here is that of George Reavis's *The Animal School: A Fable*, which goes:

> Once upon a time the animals decided they must do something heroic to meet the problems of a "new world" so they organized a school. They adopted an activity curriculum consisting of running, climbing, swimming and flying. To make it easier to administer the curriculum, all the animals took all the subjects.
>
> The duck was excellent in swimming. In fact, better than his instructor. But he made only passing grades in flying and was very poor in running. Since he was slow in running, he had to stay after school and also drop swimming in order to practice running. This was kept up until his webbed feet were badly worn and he was only average in swimming.
>
> But average was acceptable in school, so nobody worried about that, except the duck.
>
> The rabbit started at the top of the class in running but had a nervous breakdown because of so much makeup work in swimming.
>
> The squirrel was excellent in climbing until he developed frustration in the flying class where his teacher made him start from the ground up instead of the treetop down. He also developed a "Charlie horse" from overexertion and got a C in climbing and D in running. The eagle was a

problem child and was disciplined severely. In the climbing class, he beat all the others to the top of the tree but insisted on using his own way to get there.

At the end of the year, an abnormal eel that could swim exceedingly well and also run, climb and fly a little had the highest average and was valedictorian.

The prairie dogs stayed out of school and fought the tax levy because the administration would not add digging and burrowing to the curriculum. They apprenticed their children to a badger and later joined the groundhogs and gophers to start a successful private school.[xxviii]

Now, how do we bring this understanding into the classroom as we are talking about student engagement?

First Key: Intrinsic Value of Task (Motivation)

Knowing how to make a task intrinsically valuable is not easy. I recognize that. That is why let me say this: "This is not a rule or prescription; this may be worthy of consideration." In the three situations illustrated and in the animal fable, there is one thing common: *freedom to choose.* What I tried in the classroom is give the students the options of evidence that they accomplished the goal. They can make a PowerPoint presentation, a poster, an information board, video presentation, and so on. More so, I gave them options on the grade they aspire to achieve, where the threshold was meeting the standard. Below that is not a passing grade, and equal or above that are the grade categories of meeting the standard, beyond the standard, and beyond grade-level standard.

Of course, there were students who chose the least, yet there are those who chose to make the most. In the final analysis, though, it's about *meeting the standard* or *trying, at best,* to meet it. Another takeaway was I was not *pushy,* for they were given the *freedom to choose.*

By doing that, I saw the *"Empowerment"* described by Spencer and Juliani.[xxix] I saw the spectrum of student interest and drive to achieve the goal. More so, there was few to no question about their grade, for they were as well given the option on how far they wanted to go and make.

Before my dentist pursued his degree, before my kids played the dentist-patient role, before my students pursued their research undertaking and product, there was a consideration in the mind then a settlement. It's called *choice.* The core of "intrinsic value of the task" then is *choice,* specifically the *freedom to choose.* You simply cannot force anyone to do something if he did not choose it in the first place. Choice is powerful, for it is personal. They own it. It can make your students follow your classroom expectations without you asking them. It can make your students improve their academics. It can make them learn way beyond daily goals and curricular standards you aspire them to achieve. It can make your students discover and hone their own interests. Most importantly, it can make you as their teacher see the things you never thought they are capable of as they reveal their full potentials before you.

Second Key: Foster Student Agency

Student agency pertains to allowing the students to play an "active role" in their own learning.[xxx] It stands on the premise that the students are being shaped by their environment, and if they can realize that they can affect change to the environment that shapes them, they may get driven to affect the change that they can possibly do. According to the Organization for Economic Cooperation and Development (OECD),

> It (Student Agency) is about acting rather than being acted upon; shaping rather than being shaped; and making responsible decisions and choices rather than accepting those determined by others.[xxxi]

Considering the intrinsic value of the task for a student is not enough. It has to go along with allowing student "to play an active role" in "their own learning" which is consistent with what an "engaged student" is, that he "drives" his "own learning" and he will "persist" "in the face of difficulty."

What does this mean to a teacher?

Teachers are considered as "key enablers" for student agency.[xxxii] To be key enablers mean that in the classroom, we should provide the students an opportunity to set their own goals, to manage their own resources, to monitor and reflect on their progress, and to make adjustment in their actions. It's about allowing the students to create their own plan and to execute it toward the achievement of the goal. As said, "A vision without a plan is just a dream." The perspective is to allow the students to shape their own learning rather than shaping their learning.

Third Key: Provide Feedback

After tapping on our student's intrinsic motivation and allowing them to shape their own learning, there will be times that they will get stuck, get confused, or get lost. Therefore, we should provide necessary support as our students move toward the achievement of their goals.

Remember the time that you were trying to learn something, for example, how to drive. Where you are is *you don't know how to drive*, and where you want to be (your goal) is *a licensed driver*. To learn is a process, and as you go along, your instructor will tell you when to best turn the steering wheel, how to better press the gas pedal or brake, how you may better scan your environment, how you may better execute the changing of lanes, how to better park in the parking lot, and so on. In that process, where you are and where you want to be, you are receiving information on how to be better—*feedback*.

The same applies in our classroom; our students constantly need feedback to get going and get better with what they do. We can't expect them to get to where they want to be from where they are at the moment if we fail to provide it. As pointed by John Hattie and Helen Timperley, the purpose of feedback is "to reduce discrepancies between current understanding/performance and a desired goal." Knowing the importance of feedback, however, is different from actually doing it.

David Perkins provided a very helpful protocol that may help teachers provide constructive feedback to the students called the "Ladder of Feedback."[xxxiii] It has the following steps:

Step 1. *Clarify.* Ask questions of clarification about the work being reviewed.
Step 2. *Value.* Comment on the strengths of the work
Step 3. *State Concern.* Comment on your concerns about the work.
Step 4. *Suggest.* Make suggestions for improving the work.

In giving feedback, it is important that the teacher delivers it positively. When not done carefully, students may fall on tendency of fear of admitting mistakes and fear of committing future mistakes. It is, therefore, important that the teacher cultivates a classroom culture where students feel safe in making mistakes, in learning from it, and in trying again. After all, the goal is to better their performance by fostering their love for learning. The perspective is that *mistakes should be a normal part in the process of learning.*

In summary, there are three keys to student engagement: *intrinsic value of a task, foster student agency,* and *provide feedback.* The purpose of knowing these keys is to spark the student's interest in learning, make them own their learning, and foster their love for learning.

Engagement by Aspiring "Flow"

Every afternoon, in the school where I taught as a teacher who started over again, there is a ten-minute allotted time for "closing circle" before the students are dismissed from school. It's simply a check-in of how the kids felt about their day. It happens around 4:22–4:32 in the afternoon. I do not have kids by that time since my last class ends at 2:18. In those times, I get the chance to go to the classroom where I am partnered with a teacher that I'm amazed with every day. Let's call her Ms. L. Truth be told, I am not usually of so much help to Ms. L, for she handles the classroom very well. There is so much control in the classroom.

How did I say this?

Every afternoon that I step into her classroom, I would always see the students that seems to have been lost by the activities and assignments. The consciousness of students just seems to have been brought into a different world. I could say that they are *very engaged*, for you will see how they seem to be so focused with what they're doing. They don't seem to even notice me passing by. Their thoughts seem to have drifted away to another dimension. Every afternoon, I was just in awe. On many occasions, I would approach Ms. L and ask her, "What sorcery have you done to these students?" Then I will be responded with a smile and "It's not really like that before you came. I just try." Then I would usually ask myself, "What does Ms. L do that makes these students super engaged?" I got interested, and so I told myself: "I really want to figure this out."

I wanted to figure it out for the knowledge of figuring it out and improving myself (and perhaps, as I have said earlier, maybe I could share it someday). I studied, observed, practiced. I have seen its results.

To me, the students in the room of Ms. L are in a "state of flow" in the activity, the way Mihaly Csikszentmihalyi describes on how flow looks like.[xxxiv] This is the same state where writers, artists, athletes, chess players, and all others experience when they seem to unify with their crafts and activity—the experience where great men seem to have been detached from world and is having an adventure in a different dimension. This is what it means to be "in the zone" for a student.[xxxv] The students are in a hyperfocus. They are in a very high level of engagement. They are so engrossed to the activity that they lose track of time. They seem to dance to the beat of Ms. L, and Ms. L just seem to know what to do every time to make everybody dance in unison or even pull their selves back from the dreamland.

You yourself already experienced this state. Remember the time that you listened to an eloquent speaker that you feel like you were just carried out by his message. Remember the time that you watched a movie that it was so good that an hour seems to have just passed at the blink of an eye. Remember the time that you were having a long drive and that you and your car seemed to become one organism, having that total awareness of all road signs and being instinctive on how to respond. Remember the time that you played your hobby or favorite sport, that you were having so much fun that the day seemed to pass like a moment. Remember the time that you went to the parks and museums, that you were just amazed with all the works that you seem to be so immersed in the experience. You are enjoying the experience, and you lose track of time.

This is an amazing state to be aspired by teachers in the classroom—the state where students are so engaged in the classroom, the state wherein students direct all their attention and energy into something they love and value. The state where students simply do what they do for they love doing it, the state where the teacher seems to have total control over everything, the state where the teacher himself gets total involvement, loses track of time, and finds so much joy in what he does.

PERSPECTIVE 4

Eyes on the Goal

To make our students a learner of life for life—that's our goal.

Why Do We Do What We Do Every Day?

Can you recall everything you learned in history, science, mathematics, language, and other subjects? Now, were you able to use everything you learned from all the subjects you've learned to this day?

The answer is obvious. We cannot recall everything we learned, and we cannot use everything we learned in the classroom. However, it is undeniable that there remain pieces in each of these subjects that you can recall and that is of use for you—may it be knowledge, understanding, concept, skill, or even your view of things. Hence, you cannot recall everything, you cannot use everything, but you can use some of those things in life.

Does this mean that we are educating the younger generation for the same reason? That perhaps not everything would be of use to them but along the way, some of the things will be of use to them? Is this the reason why we're doing what we're doing every day?

Just like our students, we attended school to learn a variety of things from kindergarten to high school. Then we attended college and eventually landed a job. In the job, we met various challenges, and we learn from it until we get better with doing our job. Then we mentor those who came after us. After working and learning for years, we retire and, eventually, fall to the grave.

So what was the point of all those learning from our childhood to college to joining the workforce to retirement?

As you keep pushing your thoughts, you will come to a point that everything you learned will seem *meaningless*. After everything we have learned in school, about life, about the world, our life's conclusion is to fall to the grave—all of us. I don't mean to sound insane about this, but what I want to put in front of you is *the truth*—the truth that in our quest to learn and in our passion to teach, everything will just eventually seem *meaningless*.

Does this mean that there is no point in educating the younger generation?

No, there is a point.

Through learning, we were equipped with the capabilities to survive and thrive in any situation. The same applies with our students. By educating them, we are equipping them with necessary knowledge and skills to survive and thrive—whatever comes in their future. Constantly all generations learn—those ahead of teachers, the teachers, the students, and those after the students—for the purpose of helping them survive, thrive, and reaching their potentials as an individual.

Now how do we bring that perspective into our classroom?

Why do we keep teaching the students what we teach? To meet the curricular standards?

John Spencer and A. J. Juliani said,

> Our job as teachers, parents, and leaders is not to prepare kids for "something;" our job is to help kids prepare themselves for "anything."[xxxvi]

To "be prepared for anything" means to be a learner forever, for as long as they live. Such kind of individual is called "lifelong learner." Lifelong learner—a learner of life for life, a person who loves to learn! It is an individual who uses formal and informal learning opportunities to acquire more knowledge, understanding, or skills that he can use for his job or for personal development. This means that students do not only learn inside the four walls of the classroom; students also learn outside the classroom. This implies that what is learned in the classroom should have some practical use to the learner as he goes through life, directly or indirectly contributing to progress and preservation of mankind.

This aligns with the goal of United Nations for education, which goes:

> To ensure inclusive and equitable quality education and promote lifelong opportunities for all.[xxxvii]

Education should promote "lifelong learning opportunities." Whatever is learned in the classroom should have some practical use to the learner as he goes through life, indirectly contributing to progress and preservation of mankind.

Funneling everything down, we would see that in a year that we are given an opportunity to help the students prepare for their future, our very goal is to help them acquire the knowledge and skills equivalent to their level that will be of use to them throughout their lives. Our goal is to make our students "lifelong learners." We could come up with various reasons why we educate our children, such as "in preparation for the next grade level," "to make them globally competitive graduates," "to enable them to achieve their full potentials in the pursuit of their career," "to prepare them as good citizens of the country," and all reasons of similar sort; but ultimately, it's all about making them a kind of learner that they need to be as they go through life, achieving their full potentials until they fall to the grave.

Simply, we do what we do every day to make our students "lifelong learners"—lovers of learning.

Self-Direction Is the Key

The next question will be, "How can we make our students lifelong learners?" Or in a short span of time that our students are in our classroom, "How can we influence them to be a lifelong learner at the very least?"

I remember the time that I was writing my research paper, where after a thorough review of literature, I stated,

> It is imperative to realize that scholars have acknowledged self-directed learning as central to lifelong learning, where lifelong learning is the ultimate goal of the present education worldwide.[xxxviii]

It's like saying if lifelong learning is like a fluid that we cannot hold and self-directed learning is what we can in the classroom, then we must focus on making our students self-directed learners. It is what is in our reach that we can use to make our students lifelong learners.

What is self-directed learning, by the way?

Its most popular definition used to this day is that of Malcolm Knowles (1975) that goes

> A process in which individuals take the initiative, with or without the help of others, in diagnosing their learning needs, formulating learning goals, identifying human and material resources for learning, choosing and implementing appropriate learning strategies, and evaluating learning outcomes (p. 18).[xxxix]

With self-directed learning now entering the picture of this discussion, you might think that we are now getting off track, but I assure you that we are not. How? Making our students self-directed learners *in the classroom* is the way to make them lifelong learners as they go *out of the classroom.* The things they learned in the classroom, they will use it outside of the classroom. It doesn't matter if it is knowledge, skill, or attitude. In fact, what they learn outside of the classroom they bring as well inside the classroom. That's the perspective.

Now, how do we know that we are making our learners *self-directed?*

Recall that a self-directed learner is "someone who will find a way to learn something in any way he can," and a lifelong learner "has embraced the love for learning." In other words, they are capable of figuring things out on their own, and they love doing it. These premise leads to the need that our students should become *thinkers.*

Foster Their Thinking

When you try to step back of your classroom and watch your students for a moment, what do you see above their heads? Do you see questions, lightbulbs, and exchange of ideas, or do you see an empty bubble? I don't mean that you would think delusional thoughts about your students, but do you see whether their minds are truly engaged about the assignment, just playing school with you, or they are totally checked out?

Consider the findings of Peter Liljedahl when he studied ten classrooms, that about 75 to 85 percent of students are not actually thinking.[xl] He categorized these nonthinking behaviors into four, innumerably: "slacking" (not attempting the task at all), "stalling" (not attempting the task by doing legitimate off-task behaviors), "faking" (pretending to be doing the task but in reality are doing nothing), and "mimicking" (attempting or completing the task by recreating the pattern shown on the board).[xli] Correspondingly, only about 20 percent of students in a typical classroom are categorized as thinking students, which Liljedahl referred to as "trying it on their own," described as "those who put their heads down and tried to reason their way through the task based on their understanding."[xlii] Are these students familiar in your classroom?

So, the goal is to pull the students out of the nonthinking behavior category and bring them into the "thinking" group.

But how? How can we make our students try things on their own? Consider some of the key insights of Peter Liljedahl:

1. Point to the goal, not on the steps.[xliii]
2. Allow the students to navigate things on their own.[xliv]
3. Make the challenge incremental with the skills.[xlv]
4. Help the students monitor their own progress.[xlvi]
5. Grade based on evidence.[xlvii]

Build Up Their Belief in Themselves

"Thinking" should be coupled with "willpower." Why? Recall the definition of a self-directed learner: It is "a process in which individuals take the initiative." An individual takes "initiative." Without "willpower," there is no execution of the "thinking." When a student has a belief in himself, then he would have the willpower that he can accomplish and succeed in each task.

When the teacher gives an assignment, performance task, project, or situation, the students have their own belief, whether they could succeed on it or not. This is the "willpower." This is called by Albert Bandura as "self-efficacy."[xlviii] Scholars have affirmed that self-efficacy in learning influence self-directed learning and that the self-efficacy is the manifestation of a self-directed learner.[xlix] In other words,

> If the student has a strong belief in his capabilities, he will find ways to master the skill or competency with or without the help of other people.[l]

Hence, it is imperative for us to know how we may help boost our student's belief in their selves.

According to Albert Bandura, students' belief in their selves is informed by four sources, innumerably: performance accomplishment, vicarious experience, social persuasion, and physiological indexes.[li]

As teachers, we could boost our student's belief in their selves by helping them succeed in their tasks in school, whether big or small *(performance accomplishment)*. We could share inspiring stories of success and experiences of other people *(vicarious experience)*. We could give them words of encouragement. Simple compliments could help them *(social persuasion)*. We could help make them believe that their physiological state is not a hindrance for them to achieve the dreams they aspire to achieve *(physiological indexes)*. A lot of our students need to regain their belief in their selves. They seem to have lost it, for they learned how to not believe in their selves. They learned to fail over and over again, and it is our job to help them learn how to succeed over and over again.

On Fixing Our Eyes on the Goal

There was an instance where I watched a video interview to Elon Musk about how tightly he held on to his visions and not give up on his dream about production of electric cars as well as on commercializing space flights. His vision was considered ambitious, crazy, and impossible by many, but his response when he was considered as such kind of a person was always the same: "We've done it."[lii] He fixed his eyes on his goal, and he had a strong resolve that he could achieve it.

Similarly, every day we are there for our students with the end in the mind that we are preparing each of them for life. That's our goal, which some may not find realistic. That's our perspective. As pointed by Spencer and Juliani,

> Our job as teachers, parents, and leaders is not to prepare kids for "something"; our job is to help kids prepare themselves for "anything."[liii]

Fix your eyes on the goal. Place it above your curricular standards and daily objectives. Do not chase the success for your students, your classes, your school, or your district—for they will just follow. The end will justify the means. The outcome will speak of your daily efforts and intentions. Hone your students to become lifelong learners. Help them transcend toward becoming self-directed individuals. Tap on their minds by teaching them to become thinkers. Tap on their hearts by considering what they love to do. Tap on their spirit by helping them build an adamant belief in their selves. When we have already done our part in preparing our students for life, they will step out of our classroom. In the words of Lao Tzu,

> When the student is ready, the teacher appears. When the student is truly ready, the teacher disappears.[liv]

Our students will not be with us forever, but we can affect their lives forever.

Learn the Art of Listening

Desire that through your listening you can help.

Speaking, Listening, and Thinking

Conversations are part of our jobs as teachers. We fall into conversations when greeting our students in the morning, when conferring with our students who struggle in class, when mediating between students, when in a parent conference, when in a meeting with our administrators, or even during a casual time with our colleagues in the lounge. In the conversation, we may play the role of a speaker, simultaneously racing with our thoughts, thinking what we are talking about and where we are heading to. We may also be the listener who, for the most part, struggles to maintain focus while acquiring the meaning of the message is conveyed to us by the speaker. Whichever role we play, we can ascertain that we are simply doing three things in a conversation: speaking, listening, or thinking.

When speaking, we sometimes lose our "train of thought." Along with this is the utterance of the phrase "I forgot what I was thinking earlier." When listening, we are most of the time tempted *to interrupt* before the speaker even finishes what he is saying. At some instance, we are also tempted to look away and *be distracted*, for we seem to have already taken the message that the speaker is trying to convey.

Why is it so?

It is because this is our *nature*. In other words, we could naturally lose our "train of thought" when we speak, and we want *to interrupt* or *be distracted* when we listen. This is explained by Oscar Trimboli in his book *How to Listen*. He shared:

> Our speaking speed is 125 words per minute.
> Our listening speed is 400 words per minute.
> Our thinking speed is 900 words per minute.[lv]

These numbers imply three things.

First, we think faster than we speak, and so we are tempted to pass judgments, we already have a picture of what's coming next, or we simply choose to be distracted by things around us since the speaker cannot catch up with the speed of our thoughts.

Second, we listen faster than we speak—that is we have already made meaning of the message he is trying to deliver before he even finishes, and so we usually decide to interrupt the speaker so that we can respond.

Third, when it is our turn to respond or when we take over the role of a speaker, what we say is just a very small portion of what's on our mind. Note the opposite effect. When we are at the speaker's end, the value of our thinking speed is seven times more than our speaking speed, and so we are missing about six portions of our thoughts when we speak. To sum it up,

1. We think faster than we speak, and so we tend to pass judgments, anticipate, or be distracted.
2. We listen faster than we speak, and so we get tempted to interrupt.
3. When we speak, we lose portions of our thoughts, so what we say is just a little portion of the message we are trying to convey.

Listening, being in the middle of what we are thinking and what we are talking about, or vice versa of what we are talking about and what we are thinking, is therefore our way to fully get an equal understanding about the message. It is the balance in between, something that must be learned though practice, that is why listening is considered *a skill not easy to master*. Listening is a skill that requires us to *pay full attention* to what is being said and that which is not, a skill that enables us to hold our thoughts, anticipations, judgments before making any response.

Listen Actively

In listening with our students, colleagues, or other people around us, we are to remember that we should listen *actively*. It entails "that we get inside the speaker, that we grasp from his point of view just what it is he is communicating to us" according to American psychologists Carl Rogers and Richard Farson.[lvi] This means that we should try to fully understand the message that the person is trying to convey by paying attention to its two essential components: the "content" of the message as well as the "feeling" that comes along with it.[lvii] By trying to fully understand the message we are getting from the speaker, we make him feel that we genuinely respect him and we value everything he shares.

But what are the indicators that we are listening actively?

Show Evidence

We want to show to the speaker that he has our undivided attention, and so we do this by maintaining our eye contact, nodding occasionally, maintaining a welcoming posture, and responding with verbal comments of encouragement to keep going.[lviii] Showing evidence that you listen invites the speaker to remain fluid with everything that he is telling, subconsciously providing a welcoming, safe, and understanding atmosphere.[lix]

Don't Interrupt

We want the words of the speaker to keep flowing as he races with his thoughts. We know from earlier sections that once we try to interrupt, there is a huge chance that he will miss some of the things that he is supposed to say. We speak slower than we think, so the speaker is catching up with his thoughts. That is why when we ask them to continue after an interruption, we are usually met with the responses "Where was I again?" "Where did I stop?" or "I lost my train of thought." So hold yourself. Don't let your thinking speed and listening speed overcome your self-control. Allow the speaker to remain fluid.

Clarify

After the speaker has been able to pour out everything he wanted to tell, we first want to make sure that we get and understand the message from his or her perspective. How?

Rogers and Farson suggests that

> A good rule is to assume that you never really understand until you can communicate this understanding to the others' satisfaction.[lx]

We can therefore repeat what our speaker had said and confirm from the speaker that we are getting it right before we make any response.

Respond Appropriately

We listen not to judge, not to give advice, and not even to encourage someone to go in a particular direction.[lxi] Our goal is to help the speaker bring his jumbled thoughts to *order*, to make what is fuzzy *clear*, and to *shed light* to what is unseen. Through this, the speaker can connect the dots of each detail, make meaning about these connections, and stand above the grand picture of the experience. In other words, our intention should be to enable the speaker to make sound choices for himself without imposing our own opinion.

We are to share our honest opinion that will allow him to see his concern at different perspectives. From this, he can reflect on his own thoughts and experiences, examine each perspective, and anticipate possibilities of the decisions that he would make. After all, we want the resolution to be personal, originating from the speaker and not from us.

Listening Does Not Always Mean Being in a Conversation

Let me share to you some phrases:

"Mister, I was behaving well in class today. Can you tell my mom I did good today?"

"Mister, can I redo some of my assignments so that I can play in the soccer game?"

"Mister, can I show you the drawings I made?"

This is what we are certain: It's not about the behavior, not the assignments, and not the drawings. My students were communicating something else; so is our students, and we must listen to it. To listen is "to hear something with thoughtful attention."[lxii] It's an active psychological process of making meaning of the sound that we hear.

Beyond the words, it includes the behavior. In the classroom, there is a phrase known by each teacher, which goes "Every behavior is a communication." It is not just about what someone says but also what someone does not say. It's about digging deeper into the thoughts, struggles, experiences, motivations, etc., of our students. Through this, we will acquire an understanding why our students say what they say and why they behave the way they do; and from that understanding, we can possibly teach or support accordingly.

Listen to Our Students with Compassion

You don't approach any random person and speak to him for no reason. Hence, when our students approach us, it is of no accident. It means that they trust us and they feel safe with us. There are reasons why we should listen to our students: to make them feel that they are heard, to feel the experience that he is going through, and to help them alleviate the undesirable experiences that they are going through.

To listen to our students with compassion is to especially aim for the third reason—that is *to desire* that *through your listening*, you can *help* with what your student is going through. Don't mistake *listening with compassion* to an obligatory or compulsory act of sufficing your student needs through all your efforts or own resources. It may even mean not doing anything or just being there.

Way back in high school, I've read a short story titled "Just Being There." It was about someone who remained by the side of her friend facing tribulations in life. She was not doing anything, but her mere presence is a fortitude of the other. Similarly, it is not all the time that we as teachers are required to act when we listen to our students especially when they share about the adversities they have at home, in school, or with their peers. Sometimes they just need someone to listen.

"Just being there" is true in our lives. One instance, I came across a social media post from an old colleague of mine that at the end of the day, she has some students getting into her classroom after dismissal. Some need support in their assignments, but others simply need "a sister," "a friend," "a parent," or just someone who would listen. This sends us a message that there are so many things that we don't know about our students. That is why however they act in our classrooms, first we must choose to understand.

In some situations, we are urged to take action. This is especially true when the information we get may potentially cause harm to the one we listen to or to other people around him. *It is better safe than sorry*, and it is better to do it *sooner rather than later*. We can desire to help simply by requesting the support of parents, school counselors, our colleagues, or the school administrators. Sometimes the desire to help does not necessitate us to make use of personal resources; rather, simply be the courage that our students lack.

Don't Take It Personally

Sometimes we come across some students who simply vent out things out nowhere or maybe vent out noncurricular-related matters when we try to talk to them for some reason. In these instances, don't take it personally. There is a story that we can associate with this, which was that of David Pollay's "Law of Garbage Truck." It was a law he learned from his taxi driver when they almost had an accident in New York because another car from the parking space jumped into their lane. The guy yelled at them with inappropriate words, but his taxi driver just smiled at him and waved, and so he asked, "Why did you just do that?"

His driver responded:

> Many people are like garbage trucks. They
> run around full of garbage, full of frustration,
> full of anger, and full of disappointment. As their

garbage piles up, they look for a place to dump it. And if you let them, they'll dump it on you. So when someone wants to dump on you, don't take it personally. Just smile, wave, wish them well, and move on. Believe me. You'll be happier.[lxiii]

When applied to the context of our classroom, it means that we don't need to take any negative interaction that we might have with the student personally. What I mean by "negative interaction" is anything that could drain us. Save your energy, and maintain your positivity. Sometimes they just need to vent out their frustrations, anger, and disappointments; and when they do, we can simply leave it there. What they sometimes need is just a site to dump it in, and it just happened to be before you. Don't take it personally. If need be, respond or take action, but make sure to first try to have a deeper understanding of where they are coming from.

The Power of Listening

It Heals

We have students who at their early age are carrying a heavy load. As I have indicated in "Just Being There" and David Pollay's "Garbage Truck Law," our mere presence of being there as they share their problems or vent out their frustrations is enough to unload some of the burdens they are carrying. It heals by making them feel that they are heard, that there is someone who understands what they are going through, that there is someone who feels the experiences they are having, and that there is someone who desires to help and support them in any way they can.

It Builds Relationships

Listening connects two people. It breaks barriers that enable relationships to grow. In one of the professional developments I had, the speaker said, "One of the most effective ways to make your students do what you want is to build a relationship with them first." Indeed, for as said by Theodore Roosevelt,

> People don't care how much you know until
> they know how much you care.[lxiv]

Through listening, you show that you care, and that gets reciprocated with a permission to allow you to contribute to positive changes in your student's life. There is usually a fear from a teacher, though, that when the relationship is established, the student may take advantage of it. Let not that thought be a barrier. You can set the academic standards while maintaining that relationship. That is why "warm and strict" exists, for it calls that you can maintain the standard while being caring at the same time.

It Is Contagious

In listening, you practice suspending your judgment, see the perspective of the others, and closely examine the details of any situation. Consequently, it broadens your perspective and deepens your understanding about things. By lighting up their thoughts, instead of judging, advising, or encouraging, you are giving them the opportunity to carefully consider their choices, subsequently directing them to what is right at their own will. Without you knowing, you are actually affecting the lives of many, for the things you do gets subconsciously intricate to their own beings. In the words of Rogers and Farson,

> Listening behavior is contagious... Just as
> one learns that anger is usually met with anger,
> argument with argument, and deception with
> deception, one can learn that listening can be
> met with listening.

How beautiful it is to have a world that heals, where individuals build relationships and where a culture of seeing the perspectives and deep understanding is spread.

Train Self-Discipline

*The habit of making choices can be learned,
and the habit should be "the good."*

This Is Nonnegotiable

Simply, without discipline, there is no order.

Discipline refers to "the quality of being able to behave and work in a controlled way which involves obeying particular rules or standards." Hence, it is something possessed by an individual that guides his actions. *Discipline* is also described as "the practice of making people obey rules or standards of behavior and punishing them when they do not," meaning it can be facilitated by another individual, which in the classroom is the teacher. Hence, it's the teacher's task to train his students to obey the *rules or standards* for the students to (1) acquire "discipline" and (2) "maintain order" in the classroom.

Principles in Disciplining

Every student has a different background, story, need, and personalities, and discipline can sometimes be a challenge. We discipline with the end goal of helping the student acquire the skill of disciplining himself, the "self-discipline." Here are the general principles in doing that:

Discipline in Private

We praise in public, but we discipline in private. This is true anywhere—at home, in school, in the workplace, etc. That is why we do not correct our students in front of the class or in front of their friends. We always must set the right place and time to correct his behavior.

Aim to Build Integrity

The purpose of discipline is to make our students reflect on their own mistake and help him make better choices in the future. Though it primarily appeases the ones he might have wronged or it addresses some issues he might have caused, discipline in due course fortifies his integrity. In other words, it would condition him to do the right things even when no one is watching.

Seek a Mediator If Need Be

There are students who for some reasons would not initially admit their mistakes or not hold themselves accountable of their actions. The teacher can only do so much, but with the help of his colleagues, school counselor, dean of discipline, or school administrator, the matter gets resolved. In doing so, it is important that the mediation result to an understanding of perspectives, maintenance of student well-being, and restored relationship of involved parties.

Let Love and Compassion Remain

There are students who can go against every rule and authority. What I mean here are the very hard ones who just don't care about the rules and authority and that even the authorities have not figured out how to handle them. Whatever they say, whatever they do, let love and compassion remain. We do not know much about their stories and what is happening inside of them, which for some reason made them become like that. Let love and compassion remain, for usually they are the students who need it the most.

"Training" Toward Self-Discipline

There is a notion that teachers are *disciplinarians* for the consequences they implement to students who for some reason fail to follow the expectations. I propose that they be called *trainer*, for after all, they are training the students to acquire the quality called *self-discipline*. A disciplinarian's role ends with delivering the consequence while a trainer's role ends only when the skill is acquired and mastered as a habit. The principles were laid earlier as protocols to be remembered by the teacher in implementing discipline in a general sense. This next section will lay down the steps on how to train the students in a more narrowed lens. I have especially used the acronym CHOICE, for I find it very powerful in imposing discipline to our students. Choices meet your expectation without getting a stronger pushback. More so, it trains their mind to keep making better choices.

> C: Clearly set your expectations.
> H: Have regard to the root when expectations are
>   not followed.
> O: Offer choices.
> I: Ignore personal emotions.
> C: Consistently follow through your expectations.
> E: Ensure parent awareness.

Clearly Set Your Expectations

What is a clear expectation? How do we know that the expectation is clear? Let's answer that question with the help of the sample expectations below. Which of these expectations is clearer?

1. "During work, I want your voice at conversational level."
2. "During work, I want your voice at table-group level."

Let's have another one:

1. "During work, I want your voice at conversational level."
2. "During work, I want your voice not to exceed the volume of music I'm playing."

Obviously, in both examples, the second example is clearer than the first.

What makes the first not?

It is possible to have a "conversational level" of voice and still be heard by other table groups as opposed to "table group," where a boundary was drawn not to be heard by another table group. The same with "not to exceed the volume of music I'm playing" since there was a line drawn to how loud the student can get. In both examples, where expectations are clearer, there was one common element: *boundary*. Hence, we know that the expectations we set are clear when *the boundary is clear*.

Have Regard to the Root

I had one student who I had to ask to be on his assigned seat and to ask permission if he wishes to move. For many days, he just kept getting out of his seat, not asking permission, and moving to another. The motivation was he wants to be with his friends, and surely I have no objection, for it helps him finish the assignment. However, to be out of seat and not ask permission prior means not following the classroom expectation.

So, at one point, I asked him to get back to his seat, then I approached:

"I appreciate that you initiate with working on our assignment and that you are completing it, but do you know the expectation before moving out of your seat?"

He responded with "Yes."

(Oh! In my mind, he knows and he was pushing buttons?)

So I asked again: "It's good that you know. Now how do you ask?"

Then I was responded with a calm "Can I go?"

(Oh my. Do you get the picture?)

So I said, "No. Try again."

And he told me, "What do you mean? I already asked."

Then I said, "First, raise your hand," and he did. So I said, "Now, ask."

"Can I go?" he said.

Hearing that, I said, "No," and he looked frustrated already.

I told him, "When you ask, you have to address your teacher, so ask like this: 'Mister, can I go sit next to...'"

I saw realization in his face, and he did what I told him. Then, over and over again, he did what we have practiced every day. The point here is as a disciplinarian, we must first understand why the student cannot follow the expectation when it was already "clearly" set. Otherwise, we might fall easily into an interpretation that the student is pushing our boundary when it might not be the case.

As I have shown in the earlier example, the student does not intend to push buttons; he was just not taught how to ask permission *properly*. Surely there are students who intentionally push buttons, but consider this as a system similar to the *due process*. Before coming up to any conclusion, have regard to the root. Maybe the student cannot follow because he was not taught, he does not have the skills, or for other reasons of similar nature. When a student fails to follow the expectations, it is not always necessarily because he wants to challenge the teacher's authority.

Offer Choices

There are students who after you have regarded the roots show that he just really wants to challenge your authority. In delivering consequences, first offer choices. Why? Choice is powerful. It is personal. It was made from thoughtful consideration. It is a way of training the mind to consider the advantages and disadvantages of a decision. It is owned. Aside from these, choice is the key to intrinsic motivation—the drive to do the thing because one wants to do it. To sum it up, there are three reasons for offering choices:

1.   It is personal.
2.   It trains the mind to choose what is right.
3.   It taps into the intrinsic motivation of an individual.

Let me share with you an example in my classroom.

The constant use of cellphones by children is a worldwide problem. It is not surprising that it's a problem in divisions, districts, schools, and even at home. When the student does not follow the expectations about cellphone use in the classroom, I would usually give them two options: First, they hand it over to me, and I'll give it back to them at the end of the class or second, they will hand it over to the office and take it at the end of the day. They always take the first option, which means that I get what I want without nagging over it.

Offering choices is so beneficial in the long run for three reasons:

1. It teaches your students personal accountability.
2. It gives you a clear procedure on how to deal with every unmet expectation.
3. It reduces pushbacks.

Ignore Your Personal Emotions

Delivering a consequence can sometimes be challenging for a teacher especially because of the loving nature of the teacher. It is, however, written that "Whoever spares the rod hates their children but the one who loves their children is careful to discipline them."[lxv] To discipline means to love, and so consequences must be delivered. It benefits the teacher, for it maintains his authority and credibility. It benefits the student for it trains him "to obey" the "rules and standards," hence, "discipline."

Ignoring your personal emotions when delivering consequences means to strongly adhere to 100 percent; not 75, 85, 95, nor 99 but 100 percent. There should be no room for noncompliance; otherwise, the authority of the teacher will crumble. In my first months of teaching, I thought 99 percent can be "okay," one student who is not complying could be okay, but it proved to me that it is really not. I have seen its result happen through personal experience, and only then I appreciated it. In the words of Doug Lemov,

> There's one suitable percentage of students following a given direction in your classroom: 100 percent, if you don't achieve this, you make your authority subject to interpretation, situation, and motivation.[lxvi]

Consistently Follow Through Your Expectations

Delivering a consequence is a great start, but being consistent with it is much better. It requires discipline in yourself not to allow any unmet expectation slide. It is about holding on to the standard and not lowering it down for a longer time. The perspective is that the standard should remain at that level *for as long as you are their teacher.* It's having the perspective of a marathon, not a sprint; the perspective of a finisher, not a starter. Consistency with expectations is easier said than done, for it requires discipline from the trainer himself. It is training both for the trainer and the student.

Consistently following through the expectations does not mean that you stop teaching at the instant you see it. It means taking note of the unmet expectation in your head, considering the possible motivation and the degree of problem that it is causing at the moment or that it will cause in the long run, then addressing it at whatever appropriate time. It can be before teaching, during teaching, or after teaching. The point is to address any unmet expectation on whichever time it may best be addressed. It is said "whatever you allow, you promote," and so there should be no unmet expectation that is allowed and promoted.

Ensure Parent Awareness

This is the most important part of all the principles, yet not all teachers do it. Why? Some teachers don't want to deal with the parents—perhaps because it's not all the time that you get a supportive response. Whether the parents would support though or not, let them know. It is their right to know what is happening in the classroom. Let them know as soon as you observe some behavior starting to escalate, so that they may help you already on the onset. Moreover, when the time comes that you need to address it, you already have established the line to request for their support.

I found that catching potential behavior issues and partnering with the parent as soon as you can is very helpful. On the following day, you would have a student who would apologize, a student who would retreat from the negative behavior, or an opportunity to sit down with the parent to problem solve. This is so helpful, for it maintains your authority in the classroom; and for as long as you have that, you can make sure that the learning environment is conducive for all students to learn.

How about the really "hard parents"?

Surely there are. Just let them know still. Just make them aware. That's our job. Remember two things: First, you are the *second parent* and *not the first.* Second, if not through you, fate will always find a way to help the child, maybe through some other people or through other circumstances. Just let your love and belief to the child remain. We acknowledge that we have no control over everything, but let it not stop us from doing our job.

As the Trainer of Self-Discipline

First, be disciplined.

"Can the blind lead the blind? Will they not both fall into a pit?" As said.[lxvii]

Similarly, how can an undisciplined person guide another undisciplined person?

So first, be disciplined.

There are two forms of discipline—that which is imposed by others on you and that which is imposed by you on yourself. The first form is what we do so that the second may be achieved by our students—*self-discipline.* This is the quality that sets apart the best from the average, especially evident among athletes. They understand its value, and they practice it every day. Through self-discipline, their day doesn't run them; they run their day.

Hence, if self-discipline is what we aspire for our students and that we are their trainer, their model, and the authority they follow, then it is just logical that teachers should possess the greater form of discipline first, the *discipline of self,* the discipline of sticking to the standard. Without discipline, we can't do much about anything in our profession, for "discipline is the bridge between goals and accomplishment."[lxviii] Discipline is the quality that can make us finish what we started when our motivation runs out. This is the quality that could make you defeat the temptations, pleasures, and convenience that the world offers. Discipline is triumphing of what is right over what is convenient.

Forgive Seventy Times Seven Times

This is the true meaning of unconditional love.

They Do Not Know What They Are Doing

Recalling my early teaching years, I would always emphasize to my students the value of education. I would tell my personal stories and how I struggled so hard to just get through every day especially when I stepped into college. It was hard especially with a broken home. My story would then end with an emphasis on valuing education, for that is a treasure that cannot be stolen by anyone. I would emphasize the same to my students—that education is very important whether they pursue a career or other fields that interest them.

Also, I'd usually share to them what a friend of mine said to me during my college days, that "when you get to a particular age, you will see things differently." Indeed, when I reached the age of twenty, my perspective was I must be independent enough. When I reached the age of twenty-seven, I need to settle and make my own family. When I reached the age of thirty-three, my perspective was life is so short and I want to create something that I could leave as my legacy. Recently, I was told "When you reach a senior's age, you will realize that everything you worked for are useless. You will see how important it is to spend time with your children, your family." I believe so. Hence, truly people's perspective change as they age.

The point of preceding stories is that our students have a different perspective as well. Yes, they may seem to know everything, but truly there are so many things that they are yet to know. They haven't walked the path you walked. They haven't sailed on the seas you sailed. They haven't been to what is beyond their horizons. They haven't seen *yet* the things you've seen. It is our duty as their adults to understand them, guide them, and help them acquire the skills they need for life.

They can be naughty. They can be tough. They can be rude. They can be disrespectful. Know and recognize, however, *they are just kids. They do not know everything they do.* Like a child seeing a candlelight and curious of what it is, they will try to reach their fingers to it. Hold their hand if need be. Teach them what is right and wrong. Coach them how to do things right. Guide them to the better paths. Understand where they are coming from. If they make mistakes, forgive them.

In the classroom, you will meet very challenging students—those who will push your buttons, those who will push your boundaries, those who will try to get on your nerves. The key to dealing with these students are to see their perspective, understand where they are coming from, and to have an *always forgiving heart.*

Understanding Our Students

Our students' behavior is always driven by their needs. Hence, every behavior sends a message to the teacher and other people around them of what he needs. One helpful way to see this is Maslow's hierarchy of needs, which suggests that before an individual could move to the higher need, he must satisfy the lower need.[lxix] This means that the individual cannot advance to the self-fulfillment needs unless the basic need (physiological need such as food and safety need such as home) and psychological need (belongingness need such as friends and esteem need such as feeling of accomplishment) is satisfied. Hence, when a student shows misbehavior in the classroom, the student is sending a message that he has a basic need or psychological need that has to be satisfied. Subsequently, this might mean engagement issues in classroom activities and assignments.

Another way of understanding what message is being communicated by the student is through the Conscious Discipline Brain States Model.[lxx] According to the model, there are three brain states, namely survival state, emotional state, and executive state. Survival state is also described as a *"fight or flight state,"* hence, a student may demonstrate aggressive or retreating behavior. The student is sending a message that he does not feel safe. In the emotional state, the student shows unlovable behavior through her verbal reactions and nonverbal gestures. The student at this state longs for love and connection. In the executive state, student's action is more guided by his higher thinking, hence, the student is in a regulated state and demonstrates positive behavior.

In the classroom, recognizing what message is being communicated by the student is vital. It allows the teacher to have a deeper understanding of the student. Further, it allows the teacher to seek for ways to fulfill these needs with the help of parents, school counselors, and school administrators. Surely you cannot satisfy all your students in the classroom, but recognizing them is the first step to helping and supporting them to satisfy it.

What Our Students Need

Constantly I would ask myself why my kids behave the way they do. What support can we best give? How can we best support them? I want to understand them. In my quest to understand them, I have come to four things that our students need:

1. Teacher of Patience
2. Listening Ears
3. Seeing Coach
4. Proactive Second Parent

Teacher of Patience

Not a patient teacher but a *teacher of patience.* Every teacher was honed to be patient, but if any patient teacher cannot recognize the need of students to learn patience, the struggle to understand where the student is coming from will start. More so, we might misinterpret them. Simon Sinek explains that imperative to understanding the younger generation is the recognition that they grew up in a world of *instant gratification* where if they want to buy something, if they want to watch any TV show, if they want to get hold of somebody—they could get it *instantaneously.* Often, as Simon Sinek said, they are misread as *entitled* when in fact they are *impatient.*[lxxi] Simon Sinek illustrates that

It's as if they're standing at the foot of a mountain. They know exactly what they want.

> They can see the summit. What they do not see
> is the mountain.[lxxii]

Our students need someone who would help them recognize that the way to get to the summit is to journey through the mountain.

Listening Ears

Recall what I said in Perspective 5 where one time, I was scrolling on social media when I came across the post of my old colleague, where the message was that not all our students who go to school every day needs a teacher. Some of our students just need someone who will just be there to listen to them. Yes, we planned so hard prior to instructional days, but no matter how good we may have done it, if the gate through our students' mind is locked by the weight of the emotions that they bear, it will never get through. The heart is the way through the mind. As Theodore Roosevelt have said, "People do not care how much you know until they know how much you care."[lxxiii]

This reminds me of a time when one of my college professors sidetracked with life lessons when she was teaching us about the parts of the heart. She erased the letter *t* in the heart and said that for us to get to someone's heart, we need to "hear." Then, she erased letter *h* and said that this is why we were gifted by God with "ear." She proceeded with combining the shape of two pair of ears that symbolize the shape of a heart. It bears deep meaning. Sometimes listening is the least that we can do, but it is the most in the eyes of our students. Sometimes listening is even the most memorable moments for them and for us. An adage says, "We have two ears and one mouth for a reason."

Seeing Coach

It was soccer season when I was asked of favors from my most challenging students. Let me emphasize this—*my most challenging students every day.* Just imagine a 180-degree shift of how a very nonacademically engaged, always off-task student, not following the classroom expectations most of time, turning into a very calm and sweet one the following day.

"What kind of sorcery is this?" I asked. It's not just one, but all others approached at different times and said, "I really want to play the game this afternoon? I'll do everything you will ask of me." There! There the motivation revealed. Though I know that they just want me to give them an acceptable grade so that they may be eligible for the game and that I'm apparently of no use to them after that, they are telling me something worth emphasizing to every educator. Definitely we can use their grades as a motivation to get them rolling in the classroom for that season, but they are telling something deeper than this.

Seen. More than the grade, to be seen is of greater weight for them. They want to be seen. They crave for the phrase "I'm so proud of you!" They crave for the words "You're such an amazing person!" They want to be seen as someone who "everyone else would cheer" and "can be proud of." What does this mean? On season or off season, we should not take for granted the times that they have done something good. No matter how simple it may be like stacking their chair, getting a good score, helping their peer, picking up a trash, etc., a simple "good job" and "thank you for doing that" means a lot to make them feel that they are always *seen.* Big or small, we should always celebrate every good deed, good thing, and accomplishments that our students made.

Proactive Second Parent

Personally, I am not comfortable in engaging in lengthy conversations. It just seems to drain me. To communicate and collaborate with the parents is a struggle for me due to my personality. However, I learned through observations and constant reflection that when you choose the teaching profession, no matter how much you want to get away with it for any reason, to be a proactive second parent is *nonnegotiable.* Consider the need to collaborate and maintain that active line of communication with your students' parents an essential teaching tool and skill. I could say that once you grasp the need to have this, and you started to bring this to your actual practice, the dynamics of your classroom and the way you see your classroom will change dramatically.

I learned this the hard way as a teacher who started over again. I was just a reactive teacher. I only reached out when there are issues in the classroom that arise. I always catch what is negative about the student and communicate these to the parents. I was not able to take by heart the duty of being a proactive second parent—a kind of parent who gives the picture to my partners on how their kids are doing at school, what good things they did for the day or week, what discoveries I learned about them in school, what interests did they show in school, what struggles do they have, and how can we help support them and give them the best experience in school. This is about knowing the students below the surface and having connection with their home unit.

We often hear the words "Kids of this generation are really different." Have we not heard of these words when we were the kids? That *kids (we) of this generation are really different.* In the final analysis, *they are just kids.* They need love, guidance, and support from us. We must understand to teach them. To do so, let us teach them how to be patient. Let us lend listening ears when they experience struggles. Let us always see the good and hope in them. Let us be a proactive parent to them. The way to teach them is though their hearts.

Why Forgive Seventy Times Seven Times?

It was Monday, and we had a Professional Development (PD) session in the school library. At one point, our facilitator asked us to write a "note of appreciation" to three people in our building as an exercise of "cultivating the culture of positivity" and of "being seen." After giving my three note cards and reading them to my persons, my coach approached me and read to me a card that says,

> I appreciate the ways you maintain positiv-
> ity and respect for all your student even when it's
> not reciprocated by them.

More so, I received other cards that says I am always maintaining my "calm" despite my challenging students and circumstances. I was not. Let me share to you some stories.

After graduation, I started teaching in a private school where even the little noise from a student's chair I do not permit. I was a fresh graduate. I was young. They must be careful. I was strict. In other words, my classroom has always been super quiet that you cannot even hear a pin drop. There was one instance that various students made a noise, and out of my anger, I cussed at them badly. I was called to the office. Recognizing my inappropriate behavior, I apologized to my students. My students accepted my apology. My students even did the same. I never did it again for years, for I recognized the value of self-control and the better way of responding.

However, when I taught at a public school, I met a very tough student. He was known in the entire school with that image. One afternoon, I felt like I'm done with him just talking over me and engaging other students not to listen to the class, so out of impulse, I called him with an inappropriate word—a word that would break a student's heart. When I did that, he, including the entire class, remained quiet for the remaining time. Nobody knew about it except me and my class, so we just went on with the days.

Then came one day where he was involved in a commotion, and since I was there, I rushed to it to stop them, but when he saw me, I would never forget the feeling of being splashed with a bucket of water by his words. Though what he told me was not part of the commotion, I know deep within that he had that courage to say those words to me, for he was at the peak of his emotions. His words simply spilled out. I would never forget that—the feeling that I felt like I have given up on one of my students. It was sad, looking back, and I know that I needed that. Then I promised to myself that no matter how hard the situation may seem, I must try to the best of my self-awareness to hold my calm, to respond appropriately.

What does all this mean?

This means *forgiveness.*

A teacher also makes mistakes and should be understood. Forgive yourself. You cannot go back to those times that you made terrible mistakes, but you can choose to forgive yourself, learn from them, and move forward. More so, no matter how much wisdom you have right now, a time will come that you will stumble again, but what a joy and peace in heart it would bring for you if you have already forgiven yourself before it even happens. These experiences taught me that no matter how challenging the students would be, choose to *always have a forgiving heart.*

Forgive your students. Forgive your students, for they do not know what they are doing. A time in their life will come that they will realize how they could have done things better in your classroom—maybe not now, not next month, not next year, not in the next five years, but I am certain that that age of realization will come. I have seen it happen over and over again. They might not be able to go back to you and say sorry, but if you have forgiven them before they even asked for it, what a joy and peace in heart it would bring for both of you.

Have an always forgiving heart.

This is the true meaning of unconditional love—to forgive seventy times seven times.[lxxiv]

PERSPECTIVE 8

Choose Your Mentor

Your students could become the mentor that you are.

All Great Men and Women Had a Mentor

Unknown about the story of great men is a mentor. They come in different names and forms—teacher, coach, motivator, guide, adviser, educator, professor, friend, husband, wife, etc. Pause. To me, this is the way John Maxwell describes himself about what he does—"adding value to people."[lxxv] Anyone who comes alongside of you to help you grow is your mentor. They influence you for the better.

I would like to ask you to name any successful person you know. Take a moment. Now think about this—is there any person who became successful working all by themselves? If you do research about them, you will find out that every successful person you know, someone from the past or present, locally, nationally, or internationally known, may they even be your family member or relative, whoever they may be, there was always one person or more who honed them to be the best that they can possibly be. They had a mentor.

Consider the following great men and women in history and their mentors:

Albert Einstein—his mentor is Max Talmey[lxxvi]
Helen Keller—her mentor was Anne Sullivan[lxxvii]
Nelson Mandela—his mentor is Walter Sisulu[lxxviii]
Dr. Martin Luther King Jr.—his mentor is Benjamin Mays[lxxix]
Mohandas Gandi—his mentor was Gopal Krishna Gokhale[lxxx]

All great men and women have a mentor, hence, every great teacher. A mentor helps you discover the things that you haven't known you are capable before. They see your weaknesses and your strengths. They see your reasons and aspirations. They see your potentials. They help you become more, at no cost. Yes, we are gifted with the ability to learn things on our own, but more so, we are also gifted with mentors in our life to whom we could get to the best we can be. They won't force you, for they understand that the decision to be at your best should start from you. Hence, open your mind, and learn from them.

What Is a Mentor?

A mentor is someone who comes alongside the individual to help him grow and develop without necessarily molding that individual to be like himself. Mentors are there to help their students discover more about themselves, revealing their own identity and pursuing their own interests. They are great listeners who pay attention to what their students say and do not say. They help them clarify their own thoughts to come up with choices that will benefit their personal development. They have a wide encompassing wisdom, deep understanding, and unfathomable values and attitude, for they have *been there* and they have *done that.*

To be a mentor is to play the highest teacher-role in a learning situation.[lxxxi] They are "skilled" but "accessible practitioners" who "have seen it all."[lxxxii] They understand how it feels to grope with teaching strategies, instructional technologies, and classroom management as well as how to achieve an academically engaging classroom culture. They have a deep understanding of student needs and quick recognition of how to work things out, brought upon by the learnings they acquired from experiences, reflective thinking, experimentations, and self-study. These premises explain why they know how to play the various roles of a teacher and to transition from one role to another should they find it necessary.[lxxxiii,lxxxiv] They can be an authority, coach, motivator, guide, facilitator, consultant, delegator, partner, and a mentor, for they recognize that not all of their students are in the same level of readiness.[lxxxv]

The Methods of a Mentor

There are three phases at which mentors help their students grow and develop. First, they *listen totally* to learn from the student. Second, they *informally teach* through modeling, partnership, and encouragement. Third, they *think reflectively* with the end goal of helping their students discover their own way of doing things.

Listen Totally

Mentors listen to what their student says, what they feel with what they say, and the nonverbal cues they show—to learn from their student.[lxxxvi,lxxxvii] This is their way of getting into the heart and mind of their student, allowing them to see their student's perspective. It will then serve as their grounds in guiding students to discover their own identity and help them hone their own way of doing things. Here I remember my mentor once told me, "You really thought that you learned from me when in fact, it is I who learned from you." Mentoring is a two-way process of teaching and learning where both the student and the mentor benefit.

Informally Teach

Mentors teach in practical settings through modeling, demonstration, and informal conversations.[lxxxviii] The world serves as their classroom or laboratory. They know the theories behind practicalities, and they deeply understand through experience that knowing is different from doing. They know that it requires modeling and practice, and so they do it that way. This is evidenced by the fact that students, prior to the end of their senior high school years, are required to do immersion or have some practical culmination activities. Likewise in college where there is internship or apprenticeship course before finishing one's degree. Opportunities to be exposed to practical settings open the eyes of students to the challenges in practice and to how they can connect the things they learned from experience and formal education to help them address these challenges.

Think Reflectively

Mentors are reflective thinkers.[lxxxix] This is their way of broadening their understanding about the students they are teaching. They consider all factors that play around their students such as their background, their values and attitudes, their experiences, the societal factors around them, their environment, and so on, to guide their way of mentoring their student, enabling them to acquire the knowledge and skills without necessarily changing their values and attitude. In other words, they are there for their students to discover their own way of doing things. They also encourage reflective thinking to their students, subsequently making their students reflective thinkers themselves in the passing of time. Through this, the mentor empowers their students to become a mentor themselves, possessing their very own identity.

Qualities of Teachers as Mentors

We know that a mentor is someone who comes alongside anyone to help them grow and get them where they are. What qualities do they have that makes them a mentor? They (are)

> M: Model the standards and the attitude.
> E: Encourage those who have weak confidence.
> N: Nonjudgmental about everything they see.
> T: Truthful with their words and actions.
> O: Observe everything that's happening around them.
> R: Respectful to all.

Model

Teachers always strive for academic excellence in their practice, and they act according to high ethical standards. They walk their talk. They understand the weight of practice compared to theories, and so they practice. For how can they share about what they do not know? And how can they ask for what they do not do? They also model the attitude, the right way of responding to any situation rather than reacting to it. They know that directly or indirectly, their knowledge, skills, and attitude influence their students.

Encourager

En means "within." *Courage* means "the willingness to face your fears." Teachers awaken their students' courage within—to face their fears, to take a step, to have faith, to keep going, and to keep on believing that one day they will get what they want. They are there when the student needs their support. They cheer on if that's the best that they can do. Ultimately, they find joy when their students achieve their aspirations.

Nonjudgmental

They understand their role as someone who has to assess where their students are and how they may be directed toward their goals. They are seekers of opportunities for improvement. They are guides and not faultfinders. You know that that their intentions are true, for you can evidence it in their words and gestures. Whatever they say, whatever they do is an effort to get closer to their students' goals.

Truthful

Teachers understand that the first step to overcome ignorance and naiveness is to acknowledge it. There is nothing wrong with not knowing, but to stay there is a different story. Their truthfulness is sometimes misinterpreted as rude, discourteous, or impolite, unpleasing, when in fact they are just speaking their truth. Their intentions are pure. Don't even mistake their tactfulness as a sugarcoat of their true message. Their language comes from the abundance of their hearts, and so it speaks.

Observant

Sometimes students would say, "How did he see that?" Then teachers would respond, "I have eyes behind me." Familiar, right? It's not just eyes behind; it is actually *eyes and ears in every corner of the room and in all places.* They know more than everyone thought; however, they choose to act like they know nothing or so little. Teachers are observant that they know who among their students struggles the most academically and emotionally and who can do anything independently. They get clues from the behavior, responses, and outputs, and so they provide corresponding support to each of their students while at the same time making them feel safe to make mistakes and learn from it.

Respectful

Teachers always take the first step to give support to their students. At the same time, they are believers of "free will." In other words, in any response from their students, there is an inner choice where it is drawn; and so, teachers recognize that they are to do their part, at their best, for that is their duty, but there are portions that must be accomplished by the student with the help of other parties. They understand that there are various factors contributing to the dynamics around their student, their classroom, and their profession and that they have no control over everything. Teachers understand that the best they can do is maintain respect for all.

The Fruit of a Mentor

Before anyone discovers his own identity of performing things and acquiring some likeness of a mentor, first, there was a free will to become. It is not possible to acquire the likeness of a mentor unless he accepts the invitation first. An acceptance of the invitation is not just literal but also figurative, for it means that the mentee allows the teachings of his mentor to grow into his heart. In the passing of time, these teachings will prosper into his heart, vented through his words and deeds, and bear fruition to the kind of mentees he is making. It is cyclical and exponential, whether in progression or recession.

What does this mean to a teacher?

A teacher himself is the fruit of the mentor he chooses to follow. You become who your mentor is. Subsequently, your students could become the mentor that you are. The measure of a teacher is the kind of students that he produces. Knowing this truth allows us to examine within ourselves how we can become a mentor that we want our students to like to follow.

What can we do?

1. Choose the kind of mentor that you follow.
2. Accept his teachings (words, methods, modeling, etc.) into your heart.
3. Cultivate these teachings, practicing and living it every day so that yourself and your mentor becomes intertwined by his teachings.

The reputation of teachers and even of the school is known by the kind of students that they produce. Teachers are made, and so are the kind of people that our students are becoming. When we come across someone acting out, we then ask "From what school did he attend?" or "Who was his teacher?" Similarly, when we learn of someone who seem academically exceptional, we then ask, "From what school did he attend?" or "Who was his teacher?"

It is therefore imperative that we choose who we follow as our mentors, for they will determine the kind of students that we will produce.

A Mentor's Joy

What a joy,
To hear the "Congratulations!"
"You're awesome!" "You're an inspiration!"
And even the unheard "I'm so proud of you!"
What a joy,
To learn about your great story,
Remaining steadfast, enduring pains,
Weathering the storms on life, kept holding on.
What a joy,
That you finally succeeded,

Testifying that dreams do come true,
Most of all, that you remained grateful to Him.

From a distance, what a joy it is to see your students attaining their successes in life. The many congratulations, the people who show how proud they are, the stories they share, their gratefulness, and the people they inspire—all of it warms the heart of a teacher, for they remember that once in their lives, they have come alongside that kid, helped him with his difficulties, with a vision of who that kid will become.

Teachers are mentors for the lifelong influence they bring to their students through the knowledge they shared, the skills they helped build, and the wisdom they imparted in dealing with the realities of life. They never left, for even at the moment that they parted from the journey of their students, their heart and their mind remained looking after them, and it is their prayer that their students remain steadfast with their dreams, not be defeated by storms of life, and that they hold on to their faith. It is every teacher's pride and joy to see their students conquering the world as themselves. These premises compel us to choose our mentors.

Lead a "Good Life"

A teacher's way of life can influence the lives of their students and of everyone else around them.

First, Be a "Good Follower"

Good leaders are good followers; so are the good teachers.

If good teachers are good followers, then who are they following?

Everything above them that governs their actions—the law, the authorities, and their higher officials. They understand that the premise of any order comes from the deliberation that *no one is above the law,* that authorities have discussed and considered the here and there of any matter on who and what could potentially be affected before any order or resolution is made, and that their higher officers are giving orders with the best intent according to what is cascaded to them.

While some others would make complaints and criticisms, they are those who would respond that everything being ordered by their higher officials are for the best intentions of everyone and everything involved. In John Maxwell's illustration, they are those who bring the bucket of water to put out the fire while others bring out a bucket of gasoline to increase the fire. To the good teachers, complaints and criticisms are a waste of energy. As said, "He who blames others has a long way to go on his journey. He who blames himself is halfway there. He who blames no one has arrived."

Some would label them as "acting heroes," "acting smart," "acting good," and the like, for they believe that these kinds of teachers have some *personal interests.* They are not. They are the ones who are secured enough to put their pride and ego in the corner for the greater good. They are the ones who see the big picture, helping them understand the importance of doing their job extremely well to the extent of carrying some other's load when needed. They are grounded on their strong moral principles, making them secured enough, empowering, and undisturbed of others' opinions as they work and make contributions to the fulfillment of the goal.

To sum it up, good teachers are good followers in the sense that they

1. submit to authority
2. do not complain or criticize

3. put the goal above and ahead of them

Though "good teachers" are "good followers," they are *not blind followers*. As I mentioned earlier, "They are grounded on their strong moral principles." When they find it necessary to speak up for what they believe is right, they will. They are good followers, but they are not leader- and people-pleasers. They will stand their ground to the extent of giving up their role and losing their all if they find the leader's direction do not lead to the greater good. As I have pointed earlier, "They are the ones who are secured enough" and they are "undisturbed of others' opinions" for they are *followers of the "good"* aimed for the greater good. Simply, they are not blind followers because they will

1. speak up their truth when necessary and
2. leave their role along all of its benefits if it doesn't serve the greater good.

Good Teachers have COURAGE

To be courageous means to do what someone desires despite fear and danger. As I pointed earlier, to be a good follower means to speak up when necessary and leave one's role along all its benefits if it doesn't serve the greater good. In speaking up, there is a danger of being labeled as someone arrogant, and to conquer that requires courage. Being *ready to leave everything* in the organization if it does not serve the greater good and be uncertain of what life will offer after that requires even more courage. Teachers who are good followers are then those who have the courage. COURAGE of the good followers is characterized with

- *Competence.* Good teachers carry their load. They get their job done with little to no assistance, for they are solutions oriented. Sometimes they even go an extra mile to support others who lag. They are confident, skilled, knowledgeable, and experienced, aiding them to work with efficiency and effectively.

- *Observant.* Good teachers are aware of their workplace's social atmosphere. They know when to step up, be still, or back off. They have a quick recognition of people's feelings, and so they time their actions accordingly. They are also the ones who is there when any organizational need arises.

- *Upright.* Good teachers act according to moral and ethical standards. They do not allow their emotions and thinking to trample that which is virtuous. Along with this is their respect to authorities, colleagues, students, parents, and other stakeholders. Due to their uprightness, they have the courage to speak up when needed without trying to trample people's rights and emotions.

- *Resourceful.* Good teachers make use of what is available and provided to them and ingeniously find ways to suffice their additional needs. Every teacher in some ways struggle with resources, yet they always seem to miraculously get through despite these lacks. They do not allow the lack to be an excuse to do their job and help contribute to the organizational goal.

- *Attentive.* Good teachers are mindful of other people's needs. They think beyond their own and usually check in with those colleagues who might need some support. When asked, they would willingly spend their time and energy without second thought. They show concern, and they desire to always be of help to others.

- *Goal-Oriented.* Good teachers always put the organizational goal above and ahead of themselves. They never lose sight of it. They are intentional with the use of their time, energy, and resources, to always move a step closer to the fulfillment of the goal. More so, they would set aside their thoughts and emotions if it means a benefit to the greater good. They are advocates of "best ideas should win."

- *Exceptional Self-Managers.* Good teachers have a great work-life balance. It comes from the premise that they cannot perform well on their job if they will not take good care of their self and their personal lives. While delivering in the workplace is important, they do not forget that primal to that is their well-being and family needs. Hence, they thoughtfully consider how the events in their personal life would affect their work and how their work may affect their personal lives to deliver in the workplace without compromise of work-life balance.

Good Teacher's Lifestyle: 1 Percent along A-B-C

It is not easy to be a teacher. You must model academic excellence. You must strive to possess the ideal attitude. To choose to be a teacher means to commit to the good lifestyle. Yes, every teacher has flaws, but one thing is common for all: Every teacher strives to model the good lifestyle, for they know that they are one of the role models of their students—the generations that come after them.

This is about *commitment*. This requires a decision—a decision to follow through and carry through that decision. This reminds me of a life story shared by a friend. Once he immersed himself into all kinds of vices and illegal activities, seeking for the meaning of his life. He never found it. Finding his existence meaningless, he tried to drug himself to end it. He failed, and during those same moments, he was called and found his purpose. In that calling, he found the true meaning of love, joy, and the meaning why he must go through what he went though. Today he is transforming the lives of those his influence touch through his testimonies. He decided. Every day he is living the new life he chose and committed to.

The same character is demonstrated by every "champion teacher." They have committed themselves to whatever is *good*, whatever is *right*, and whatever is *excellent* every day. Recall one great teacher you know or find and observe one, and you will notice that everything that seemed so hard, so challenging, so uphill to beginning teachers seemed so easy and executed so smoothly by them. They don't fight the battle to slack or underperform. They don't struggle to wake up every day and drag themselves to school. They don't struggle to step forward if there is a need to take the lead. The reason behind is simple: Doing good, choosing what is right, and performing with excellence is intertwined to their daily lives that they simply know what to do and how to do it whatever the circumstance is. This is the lifestyle they chose. It all started with their commitment.

Perhaps the poem of Mother Teresa of Calcutta best embodies the commitment to a good lifestyle for every teacher no matter what the circumstance. It says,

> Do good anyway…You see, in the final analysis… It was never between you and them anyway.[xc]

In your quest to follow though and carry through the good lifestyle as a teacher, consider this truth:

1 Percent. Recognize it. Accept It.

An adage says, "Shoot for the moon so that when you fail, you land among the stars."[xci] Champion teachers simply give their best every day, more than the 100 percent required by their calling, but they recognize as well that no matter how much they give, there will always be room for improvement. Even the laws of physics agree that practically machines can never achieve 100 percent efficiency.[xcii] One percent reminds us that there will always be a room for improvement, no matter how great someone is and no matter how hard you strive to achieve perfection. Hence, it is important that you recognize it.

Next, accept the 1 percent. This especially struck me when during the midyear evaluation with my administrator, I shared how I struggled with how to best support my students academically and how to implement some of my classroom expectations in terms of their behavior. There is just so much to consider in terms of their demographics, accommodations, and needs. Even with figuring out the best seating chart, I struggled. Then I would never forget it when my administrator told me, "I feel where you're coming from. I have been teaching for fifteen years now, and it took me 'forever' to figure everything out in the classroom." Perhaps we may consider that those words were said to simply validate what any teacher struggles with, but undeniably, it bears timeless truth. Wasn't it said that when you choose to teach, you will be a student forever?

Every student has a different interest. Every student has a different learning preference. Every student has a different upbringing. Every student has a different home dynamic. Every student has a different story. There are just so many things that are out of your control. Give your best, but accept this truth. Accept this 1 percent.

As you wake up each morning, get to school, be in the classroom, deal with your students and their parents, work with your colleagues and administrators, may your actions be guided by the following ways of looking at things:

Always Have a Positive Outlook

You are your habit. If you always choose to see the bad side of things, you lose sight of the good things. If you always choose to hate people and circumstances, then you lose sight of the loving perspective. Pessimism and optimism are both products of our habit. The former will always tell you that there is one way—give up; you're done. The latter will always tell you that there are infinite number of ways to turn any circumstance to your favor. It will give you the wisdom to make sound decisions—even in irremediable, irreparable, and impossible circumstances—so that you may emerge victorious. This mindset will make you win in every challenge that you will encounter in the profession even if it may appear that you were defeated. In seeing the good in everything, you will never feel that you have lost in anything.

Be Kind

Take a moment to remember the feeling when someone showed an act of kindness. Maybe that someone shared to you some food, gave you an unexpected gift, or simply asked you about how you have been doing. Remember that feeling. They are an inspiration of kindness. Now just imagine how your simple acts of kindness could impact your students, your students' home unit, your colleagues, your administrators, and so on. How wonderful it is to be the teacher that "gives light to everyone and whose light shines before others."[xciii]

Be kind, for when you sow kindness, you will eventually reap kindness—even much better when you share seeds of kindness that may be sown by others so that it may be planted into the deserted heart of all others. Your chain of planting and passing on kindness to other people will come back to you in ways you never will never know. This is the same in our profession, even in our personal lives.

Choose to Serve

Serving others does not mean that you will be the kind of teacher that pleases everybody. It means giving what you have, sharing what you know, imparting your skills, just helping others who need you to the best of your ability. Serving other people will open your mind to a realization that there is more to all knowledge, power, and wealth that the world can offer. It gives your life a sense of purpose. In Mahatma Gandhi's words:

> The best way to find yourself is to lose yourself in the service of others.[xciv]

Good Teacher's Self-Preservation: EnD

When you get to the library of our school, a large printed quote by Vince Lombardi will greet you. It says, "Once you learn to quit, it becomes a habit."[xcv] This is not about any teacher quitting from one school and moving to a different school. This is about the teachers who remained, trying, striving, growing every day—no matter what the circumstance. There is a difference between someone who quit the job or moved to another school and someone who totally took his feet off the teaching profession. The former is choosing to get up every time he stumbles, gets beaten, and who will definitely master the craft in the end! The latter—perhaps he was called to serve another purpose.

To be a servant, to grow, aspire for flow, fix your eyes on the goal, to learn the art of listening, to train self-discipline, to forgive, and to lead the good lifestyle every day are perspectives that are intertwined to the being of champion teachers. These perspectives are a result of huge character that a champion dwells in them. Champion teachers see far beyond others, and they recognize that *there is no end.* Recognizing that there is no end, how will you be able to sustain everything?

Encircle Yourself with the Right People

Encircle yourself with people who support and cheer you up. People around you can do two things: they may inspire you by giving you a positive outlook in life, or they may drain your energy by feeding you with negativities in everything.

There are two indicators for you to easily distinguish if the person qualifies to the former or to the latter. First, by listening to what they are saying. Their words are food for your thoughts. Hence, for you to remain inspired, full of zeal and enthusiasm, you must choose the right people, who give food for your thoughts. While it may appear true that you cannot get away from people who feed negativities to others, the fact remains that you have the choice to either shut or open the door of your thoughts to everything they say. The decision is always up to you. To be a good teacher, surround yourself with good people.

Second, the way people walk their talk. People who genuinely support you, believe in you, and love you will always be with you even at your lowest. They will always be there to help you see the good things about your circumstances. They will be there to make you believe in your capabilities again, for they believe in you. They are the ones who genuinely share your joy in your victories, for they are happy for you, and they are very proud of you. There is consistency with what they say to you and what they do or could do for you.

Do Not Forget Yourself

It is never selfish to care for the person who unconditionally offers everything to you so that the desires of your heart may be fulfilled. Remember this: "The magnitude of help that you could extend to others is preceded by the magnitude of help you can do for yourself."

Teachers too often forget their selves. Look at yourself in the mirror. Have you been taking good care of that person? No one else could take good care of that person better than you. You know that person inside-out far better than anyone else. That person deserves your care. If only you could say something to that person, what would it be? If only you could give something to that person, what would it be? Say it. Give it. Just like the way you care, advise, and give something to your students and to other people, that same person needs it.

Good Teachers Affect Eternity

Your students will come and go. Some may remember you, some may not. If life allows, your paths may cross again. Your memory might fail you to remember them. They might greet you, or for some reasons they may not. One thing will remain certain through the end though: That once in your lives, your paths have crossed; and in one way or another, you have influenced their lives as their teacher. You have a portion dwelling inside of them.

You may not be the best teacher of your students—keep giving your best though—and yes, you are just one of the eight teachers that your students have in a day and in a year and just one of the 144 teachers that he could possibly have in his fourteen years of education, yet like a mustard seed, you can never tell how huge that little influence you made could work in his life and benefit those he will meet in his life. Teachers affect eternity.

You affect eternity.

—

CONCLUSION

Perspective is our way of looking and understanding things in our classroom and in our profession. The book broadens our understanding on our role in the classroom as a teacher and offers us insights on how we can achieve these perspectives. More so, it allows us to see the meaning of why we do what we do every day. It directs our attention and resources to a purpose—the greater good and the lasting good. Truly every teacher has a different perspective from one another, but there are three things common to them: First, "All teachers desire that their students would love learning." Second, "All teachers want the best for their students." Third, "All teachers have affected the lives of those they touched in one way or another." These are undebatable.

The perspective about "To Teach Is to Serve" helps us understand that teaching is a calling, a calling that not everyone has the skill and fortitude to handle. The perspective about "Strive to Grow" helps us see that to foster an attitude of learning for our students, we should have the same attitude toward learning. The perspective about "Aspire for Flow" helps us see the path for our students to optimal experience of engagement. The perspective about "Eyes on the Goal" helps us see the significance of knowledge, skills, and attitude that we try to teach to our students every day. The perspective about "Learn the Art of Listening" helps us see the power of listening and how we should act, interact, and maintain our attitude in every message. The perspective about "Train Self-Discipline" helps us understand why we discipline our students—that is, they would have a "discipline" of their "self." The perspective about "Forgive Seventy Times Seven Times" helps us see importance of embracing mistakes as a means for learning for our students and even for ourselves. The perspective about "Choose Your Mentor" helps us see that the kind of mentor we follow affects the kind of individuals we are becoming, subsequently the kind of students we produce, so we must choose who we follow. The perspective of "Lead a Good Life" helps us see that our students come and go, even our colleagues, administrators, and all others around us; and while we are dwelling at the same point in our lives, our way of life can be a positive influence on theirs.

May these perspectives guide you as you journey down to the path of your calling.

NOTES

Perspective 1

[i] "Ancient Egyptian Servants," *Discovery Education*, accessed June 8, 2024, https://streaming.discoveryeducation.com/braingames/iknowthat/Stickerbook/sbr/Ancient%20Egypt/Royalty%20&%20Soldiers/DiscoverMore/RoyalFanner.htm#:~:text=Servants%20belonged%20to%20the%20lowest,most%20of%20the%20hard%20work.&text=Depending%20on%20the%20needs%20of,for%20children%20in%20wealthy%20families.

[ii] "Slaves and Servants in the Time of Jesus – History and Culture," *American Bible Society*, accessed June 8, 2024, https://bibleresources.americanbible.org/resource/slaves-and-servants-in-the-time-of-jesus-history-and-culture.

[iii] "Servant or Slave?" *Grace to You*, accessed June 8, 2024, https://www.gty.org/library/sermons-library/GTY129/servant-or-slave.

[iv] Matthew 21:28–32.

[v] John C. Maxwell, *The 21 Irrefutable Laws of Leadership: Follow Them and People Will Follow You* (Nashville: HarperCollins Leadership, 2007).

[vi] Elizabeth Perry, "What's Integrity in the Workplace and Why Is It Important? (+Examples)," *BetterUp*, accessed June 9, 2024, https://www.betterup.com/blog/integrity-in-the-workplace.

[vii] Matthew 13:1–17.

Perspective 2

[viii] Carol Dweck, "Carol Dweck Revisits the Growth Mindset," *Education Week* 35, no. 5 (2015): 20–24.

[ix] Junfeng Zhang, Elina Kuusisto, and Kirsi Tirri, "How Teachers' and Students' Mindsets in Learning Have Been Studied: Research Findings on Mindset and Academic Achievement," *Psychology* 8, no. 9 (2017): 1363.

[x] Bruce Lee, "Empty Your Cup So That It May Be Filled; Become Devoid to Gain Totality," accessed June 9, 2024, https://www.goodreads.com/quotes/48714-empty-your-cup-so-that-it-may-be-filled-become#:~:text=Sign%20Up%20Now-,Empty%20your%20cup%20so%20that%20it%20may,become%20devoid%20to%20gain%20totality.

[xi]   Ovid, "Dripping Water Hollows Out Stone, Not Through Force, but Persistence," accessed May 25, 2024, https://www.goodreads.com/quotes/28100-dripping-water-hollows-out-stone-not-through-force-but-through.

[xii]   Jim Rohn, "Discipline Means Doing What Needs to Be Done Even When You Feel Like Not Doing It," accessed May 24, 2024, https://www.youtube.com/watch?v=TkguYenRpps.

[xiii]   Aneko Yusagi, accessed May 31, 2024, https://www.goodreads.com/quotes/10189812-it-s-better-to-regret-trying-and-failing-than-to-regret.

[xiv]   Napoleon Hill, "Thoughts Are Things," accessed May 24, 2024, https://www.goodreads.com/quotes/732139-thoughts-are-things-and-powerful-things-at-that-when-they.

[xv]   Henry Ford, "Whether You Think You Can or Think You Can't, You're Right," accessed May 24, 2024, https://www.goodreads.com/quotes/978-whether-you-think-you-can-or-you-think-you-can-t--you-re.

Perspective 3

[xvi]   Phillip C. Schlechty, *Engaging Students: The Next Level of Working on the Work* (John Wiley & Sons, 2011).

[xvii]   Ayrton Eldridge, "How PBL Creates Authentic Student Engagement — PBL Curriculum," *Cura Education*, February 7, 2022, https://www.curaeducation.com/best-practice/how-pbl-creates-authentic-student-engagement. Accessed May 13, 2022. As cited by Mandala Barab (2022), *Engagement as Ecology of Learning* (Routledge; Taylor and Francis Group), retrieved June 1, 2024, from https://www.routledge.com/blog/article/engagement-as-ecology-of-learning.

[xviii]   Phillip C. Schlechty, *Engaging Students: The Next Level of Working on the Work* (John Wiley & Sons, 2011).

[xix]   Mihaly Csikszentmihalyi and Mihaly Csikzentmihaly, *Flow: The Psychology of Optimal Experience*, vol. 1990 (New York: Harper & Row, 1990), 71.

[xx]   Unleashing Personal Potential, Week 8 – Engagement Introduction (Flow Activity), retrieved June 2, 2024, from https://www.unleashingpersonalpotential.com.au/week-8-engagement-introduction-20#:~:text=Flow%20is%20the%20peak%20experience,%E2%80%9D%20(Csikszentmihalyi%2C%202013).

[xxi]   An informal idiom equivalent to "Flow," retrieved May 27, 2024, from https://dictionary.cambridge.org/us/dictionary/english/in-the-zone.

[xxii]   Unleashing Personal Potential, Week 8 – Engagement Introduction (Flow Activity), retrieved June 2, 2024, from https://www.unleashingpersonalpotential.com.au/week-8-engagement-introduction-20#:~:text=Flow%20is%20the%20peak%20experience,%E2%80%9D%20(Csikszentmihalyi%2C%202013).

[xxiii]   C. Whitson and J. Consoli, "Flow Theory and Student Engagement," *Journal of Cross-Disciplinary Perspectives in Education* 2, no. 1 (2009): 40–49.

xxiv   David J. Shernoff, Mihaly Csikszentmihalyi, Barbara Shneider, and Elisa Steele Shernoff, "Student Engagement in High School Classrooms from the Perspective of Flow Theory," *School Psychology Quarterly* 18, no. 2 (2003): 158.

xxv   Phillip C. Schlechty, *Engaging Students: The Next Level of Working on the Work* (John Wiley & Sons, 2011).

xxvi   Ayrton Eldridge, "How PBL Creates Authentic Student Engagement — PBL Curriculum," *Cura Education*, February 7, 2022, https://www.curaeducation.com/best-practice/how-pbl-creates-authentic-student-engagement. Accessed May 13, 2022. As cited by Mandala Barab (2022), Engagement as Ecology of Learning (Routledge; Taylor and Francis Group), retrieved June 1, 2024, from https://www.routledge.com/blog/article/engagement-as-ecology-of-learning.Engagement as Ecology of Learning. Routledge; Taylor and Francis Group, retrieved on June 1, 2024 from https://www.routledge.com/blog/article/engagement-as-ecology-of-learning

xxvii   Howard Gardner, "Multiple Intelligences" (1993).

xxviii   George Reavis, *The Animal School: A Fable* (1940), retrieved June 22, 2024, from https://greatresultsteambuilding.net/wp-content/uploads/2014/11/The-Animal-School-Fable.pdf.

xxix   John Spencer and A. J. Juliani, Empower (2017).

xxx   Maureen O'Rourke and Penny Addison, "What is Student Agency," *Ed Partnerships International* 2 (2017).

xxxi   Organization for Economic Cooperation and Development (OECD), *Conceptual Learning Framework: Student Agency for 2030,* retrieved June 3, 2024, from https://www.oecd.org/education/2030-project/teaching-and-learning/learning/student-agency/Student_Agency_for_2030_concept_note.pdf.

xxxii   Howard Gardner, "Multiple Intelligences" (1993).

xxxiii   David Perkins, *King Arthur's Round Table: How Collaborative Conversations Create Smart Organizations* (Hoboken, NJ: John Wiley & Sons, Inc., 2003).

xxxiv   Phillip C. Schlechty, *Engaging Students: The Next Level of Working on the Work* (John Wiley & Sons, 2011).

xxxv   Ayrton Eldridge, "How PBL Creates Authentic Student Engagement — PBL Curriculum," *Cura Education*, February 7, 2022, https://www.curaeducation.com/best-practice/how-pbl-creates-authentic-student-engagement. Accessed May 13, 2022. As cited by Mandala Barab (2022), *Engagement as Ecology of Learning* (Routledge; Taylor and Francis Group), retrieved June 1, 2024, from https://www.routledge.com/blog/article/engagement-as-ecology-of-learning.

Perspective 4

xxxvi   John Spencer and A. J. Juliani, *Empower* (2017), 11–20.

xxxvii   United Nations, "Goal 4: Ensure inclusive and equitable quality education and promote lifelong learning opportunities for all," retrieved May 28, 2024, from https://sdgs.un.org/goals/goal4.

xxxviii   Joenel D. Coros and Dennis V. Madrigal, "Self-directed learning, self-efficacy in learning, and academic motivation of public senior high school students," *Asian Journal of Education and Social Studies* 21, no. 2 (2021): 19–34.

xxxix   Malcolm S. Knowles, *Self-directed Learning: A Guide for Learners and Teachers* (1975), 18.

xl   Peter Liljedahl, *Building Thinking Classrooms in Mathematics, Grades K–12: 14 Teaching Practices for Enhancing Learning* (Corwin Press, 2020), 11.

xli   Ibid., 7–10.

xlii   Ibid., 10.

xliii   Ibid., 19–35.

xliv   Ibid., 133–141.

xlv   Ibid., 145–166.

xlvi   Ibid., 231–250.

xlvii   Ibid., 253–277.

xlviii   United Nations, "Goal 4: Ensure inclusive and equitable quality education and promote lifelong learning opportunities for all," retrieved May 28, 2024, from https://sdgs.un.org/goals/goal4.

xlix   Joenel D. Coros and Dennis V. Madrigal, "Self-directed learning, self-efficacy in learning, and academic motivation of public senior high school students," *Asian Journal of Education and Social Studies* 21, no. 2 (2021): 19–34.

l   Joenel D. Coros and Dennis V. Madrigal, "Self-directed learning, self-efficacy in learning, and academic motivation of public senior high school students," *Asian Journal of Education and Social Studies* 21, no. 2 (2021): 19–34.

li   Albert Bandura, "Self-efficacy mechanism in human agency," *American Psychologist* 37, no. 2 (1982): 122.

lii   Interview with Elon Musk, retrieved on May 29, 2024, from https://www.youtube.com/watch?v=8P8UKBAOfGo (0:00-0:18)

liii   John Spencer and A. J. Juliani, *Empower* (2017), 11–20.

liv   Lao Tzu, "A quote by Lao Tzu," retrieved May 28, 2024, from https://www.wolverton-mountain.com/articles/learning-from-lao-tzu.html#:~:text=Lao%20Tzu%20wrote%20that%20%E2%80%9CWhen,think%20what%20Lao%20Tzu%20said.

Perspective 5

lv   Oscar Trimboli, *How to Listen*, cited by Catherine Ducharme, "Talk Less. Do Less. Listen More. Reprioritizing Listening," 2023, retrieved June 8, 2024, from https://www.fluencyleadership.com/2023/10/11/talk-less-do-

less-listen-more-reprioritizing-listening/#:~:text=Our%20speaking%20
speed%20is%20125,than%20the%20speaker's%20talking%20speed.

lvi   Carl Ransom Rogers and Richard Evans Farson, *Active Listening* (Industrial Relations Center, University of Chicago, 1957).

lvii   Carl Ransom Rogers and Richard Evans Farson, *Active Listening* (Industrial Relations Center, University of Chicago, 1957).

lviii   Mind Tools Ltd., *Active Listening*, retrieved June 9, 2024, from https://www.mindtools.com/az4wxv7/active-listening.

lix   Mind Tools Ltd., *Active Listening*, retrieved June 9, 2024, from https://www.mindtools.com/az4wxv7/active-listening.

lx   Carl Ransom Rogers and Richard Evans Farson, *Active Listening* (Industrial Relations Center, University of Chicago, 1957).

lxi   Carl Ransom Rogers and Richard Evans Farson, *Active Listening* (Industrial Relations Center, University of Chicago, 1957).

lxii   Carl Ransom Rogers and Richard Evans Farson, *Active Listening* (Industrial Relations Center, University of Chicago, 1957).

lxiii   David Pollay, *The Law of the Garbage Truck: How to Stop People from Dumping On You*, retrieved June 10, 2024, from https://www.proctorgallagherinstitute.com/2210/the-law-of-the-garbage-truck.

lxiv   Theodore Roosevelt, "People don't care how much you know until they know how much you care," retrieved May 30, 2024, from https://www.goodreads.com/quotes/34690-people-don-t-care-how-much-you-know-until-they-know.

Perspective 6

lxv   Proverbs 13:24.

lxvi   Doug Lemov, *Teach Like a Champion* (Jossey-Bass, 2010), 168.

lxvii   Luke 6:39.

lxviii   Jim Rohn, "Discipline is the bridge between goals and accomplishment," retrieved June 5, 2024, from https://www.brainyquote.com/quotes/jim_rohn_109882.

Perspective 7

lxix   Saul McLeod, *Maslow's Hierarchy of Needs, Simply Psychology*, retrieved June 5, 2024, from https://www.simplypsychology.org/maslow.html.

lxx   Conscious Discipline, *The Conscious Discipline Brain State Model*, retrieved June 5, 2024, from https://consciousdiscipline.com/methodology/brain-state-model/#:~:text=Our%20multidisciplinary%20approach%20surpasses%20behavioral,Paul%20MacLean%2C%20and%20Alexander%20Luria.

lxxi   Simon Sinek, *Most Leaders Don't Even Know the Game They're In*, TEDx speech, retrieved May 29, 2024, from https://www.youtube.com/watch?v=RyTQ5-SQYTo, 18:08–18:47.

lxxii   Ibid., 19:44–19:51.

lxxiii   Theodore Roosevelt, "People don't care how much you know until they know how much you care," retrieved May 30, 2024, from https://www.goodreads.com/quotes/34690-people-don-t-care-how-much-you-know-until-they-know.

lxxiv   Matthew 18:21–32.

Perspective 8

lxxv   John C. Maxwell, *The 21 Irrefutable Laws of Leadership: Follow Them and People Will Follow You* (HarperCollins Leadership, 2007).

lxxvi   Ravin JG, "Albert Einstein and His Mentor Max Talmey," *The Seventh Charles B. Snyder Lecture, Doc Ophthalmol* 94, no. 1–2 (1997): 1–17, doi: 10.1007/BF02629677. PMID: 9657287.

lxxvii   Debra Michals, *Helen Keller, National Women's History Museum*, 2015, retrieved June 2, 2024, from https://www.womenshistory.org/education-resources/biographies/helen-keller#:~:text=Ultimately%2C%20she%20was%20referred%20to,her%20finger%20on%20Keller's%20palm.

lxxviii   South Africa Online, *Nelson Mandela and Walter Sisulu*, 2024, retrieved June 2, 2024, from https://southafrica.co.za/nelson-mandela-and-walter-sisulu.html.

lxxix   Stanford University, *The Martin Luther King, Jr. Research and Education Institute. Mays, Benjami*, n.d., retrieved June 2, 2024, from https://kinginstitute.stanford.edu/mays-benjamin-elijah#:~:text=Described%20by%20Martin%20Luther%20King,until%20King's%20death%20in%201968.

lxxx   India Today, *Remembering Gopal Krishna Gokhale: Gandhi's Political Guru*, n.d., retrieved June 2, 2024, from https://www.indiatoday.in/education-today/gk-current-affairs/story/gopal-krishna-gokhale-309510-2016-02-19.

lxxxi   W. Christopher Brandt, "Measuring Student Success Skills: A Review of the Literature on Self-Directed Learning," *21st Century Success Skills*, National Center for the Improvement of Educational Assessment (2020).

lxxxii   Sarah Gonser, "The Qualities of Exceptional Mentor Teachers," retrieved June 13, 2024, from https://www.edutopia.org/article/qualities-exceptional-mentor-teachers/.

lxxxiii   Sarah Gonser, "The Qualities of Exceptional Mentor Teachers," retrieved June 13, 2024, from https://www.edutopia.org/article/qualities-exceptional-mentor-teachers/.

lxxxiv   Debra Meyer, "What Makes a Great Mentor?" *Elmhurst University*, 2021, retrieved June 13, 2024, from https://www.elmhurst.edu/blog/teacher-mentor/.

lxxxv   W. Christopher Brandt, "Measuring Student Success Skills: A Review of the Literature on Self-Directed Learning," *21st Century Success Skills*, National Center for the Improvement of Educational Assessment (2020).

[lxxxvi] Sarah Gonser, "The Qualities of Exceptional Mentor Teachers," retrieved June 13, 2024, from https://www.edutopia.org/article/qualities-exceptional-mentor-teachers/.

[lxxxvii] Debra Meyer, "What Makes a Great Mentor?" *Elmhurst University*, 2021, retrieved June 13, 2024, from https://www.elmhurst.edu/blog/teacher-mentor/.

[lxxxviii] Sarah Gonser, "The Qualities of Exceptional Mentor Teachers," retrieved June 13, 2024, from https://www.edutopia.org/article/qualities-exceptional-mentor-teachers/.

[lxxxix] Sarah Gonser, "The Qualities of Exceptional Mentor Teachers," retrieved June 13, 2024, from https://www.edutopia.org/article/qualities-exceptional-mentor-teachers/.

Perspective 9

[xc] Mother Teresa, "Mother Teresa's Anyway Poem," retrieved May 27, 2024, from https://www.goodreads.com/quotes/7969043-mother-teresa-s-anyway-poem-people-are-often-unreasonable-illogical-and.

[xci] Norman Vincent Peale, "Shoot for the moon. Even if you miss, you'll land among the stars," retrieved May 27, 2024, from https://www.goodreads.com/quotes/4324-shoot-for-the-moon-even-if-you-miss-you-ll-land.

[xcii] "Why is a machine not 100% efficient?" retrieved May 28, 2024, from https://www.goodreads.com/quotes/4324-shoot-for-the-moon-even-if-you-miss-you-ll-land.

[xciii] Matthew 5:14–16.

[xciv] Mahatma Gandhi Quotes, BrainyQuote.com, BrainyMedia Inc, 2024, https://www.brainyquote.com/quotes/mahatma_gandhi_150725, accessed May 31, 2024.

[xcv] Vince Lombardi, "The difference between a successful person and others is not a lack of strength, not a lack of knowledge, but rather a lack in will," retrieved May 28, 2024, from https://www.brainyquote.com/quotes/vince_lombardi_151245.

ABOUT THE AUTHOR

Father. Husband. Brother. Son. Teacher.

Joenel Dicen Coros is a Filipino teacher who hails from Cadiz City, Negros Occidental, Philippines. He earned his bachelor's degree in secondary education major in general science from the Philippine Normal University in Visayas. After graduation, he started his teaching career at Living Stones International School, Inc., Bacolod City, a private school in the metro area of his province. After a couple of years, he served as a public school teacher in his hometown, Cadiz City, Negros Occidental. He initially served at Tiglawigan National High School, located in the suburbs of the city. Then after more than two years, he went to serve Dr. Vicente F. Gustilo Memorial National High School for seven years, handling general sciences, physics, and practical research. He also holds a master's degree in education major in physics and a Doctor of Philosophy in education major in educational management, both earned from the University of Negros Occidental—Recoletos, Bacolod City. At present, he teaches core sciences to middle school students in Colorado, United States of America.

He is the eldest among eight siblings. He is married to Mishel Panes Coros, an English Teacher, and they are blessed with two sons.